THE
POWER
OF
STORIES

A GUIDE FOR LEADING MULTIRACIAL AND MULTICULTURAL CONGREGATIONS

JACQUELINE J. LEWIS

Abingdon Press
Nashville

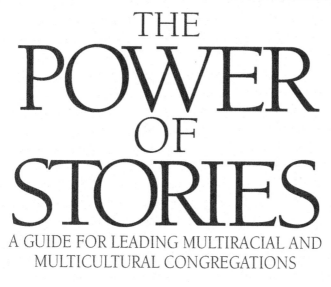

THE POWER OF STORIES

A GUIDE FOR LEADING MULTIRACIAL AND MULTICULTURAL
CONGREGATIONS

Copyright © 2008 by Abingdon Press

All rights reserved.

This book is printed on acid-free paper.

Library of Congress Cataloging-in-Publication Data

Lewis, Jacqueline Janette, 1959-
    The power of stories : a guide for leading multiracial and multicultural congregations / Jacqueline J. Lewis.
        p. cm.—(Discoveries)
    Includes bibliographical references (p.   ) and index.
    ISBN 978-0-687-65069-9 (binding: pbk., adhesive, perfect : alk. paper)
    1. Christian leadership—Case studies.   2. Multiculturalism—Religious aspects—Christianity—Case studies.   3. Race relations—Religious aspects—Christianity—Case studies.   I. Title.

    BV652.1.L483 2008

    253—dc22
                                                                    2007049664

Some appendix material also appears in Lovett H. Weems Jr.'s *Church Leadership* (Nashville: Abingdon Press, 1993). Used by permission.

08 09 10 11 12 13 14 15 16 17—10 9 8 7 6 5 4 3 2 1

MANUFACTURED IN THE UNITED STATES OF AMERICA

To my parents, Emma and Richard, who taught me that *different* and *special* were synonyms; to my colleagues at the Alban Institute and in this study, who created space for wise and candid storytelling and study; to Gordon Dragt and my Middle Collegiate Church family, who let me preach what I strive to practice; and especially to John, who reminds me daily that love is transformative and as essential as air.

CONTENTS

1. Stories and Living Texts 1

2. Storying an Ethic of Truth Telling and Social Justice . . . 19

3. Storying an Ethic of Conflict and Border Crossing 41

4. Stories on the Border 61

5. Enacting the Pentecost Paradigm 79

Appendix A 119

Appendix B 127

Appendix C 131

Appendix D 133

Appendix E 135

Selected Bibliography 141

Notes 149

CHAPTER 1

STORIES AND LIVING TEXTS

INTRODUCTION

From the first century, the church's mission has been to be the Body of Christ in the world. As such, we are called to be peacemakers; to break down the dividing walls of hostility, suspicion, fear, and prejudice; and to rehearse the reign of God on earth in our communities each day. Yet studies show that over 90 percent of American Christians worship in congregations in which 90 percent or more of the congregants there are like them (Chaves, 1999). Why is this true? In an increasingly multicultural America, and in an ever-shrinking global community, how can the church do ministry on this new religious frontier?

I am convinced that this is a question of leadership. *Prophetic, purposeful, visionary leadership by courageous, compassionate, convicted leaders can grow and sustain congregations that reflect the rich diversity of God's reign.* Leaders can, through their preaching, teaching, and developing other leaders, *story a compelling vision* in which cultural diversity is an ethical and moral imperative in the present, not a heaven-bound hope for the future.[1] Although it is true that less than 5 percent of the three hundred thousand Christian congregations in America are intentionally multiracial and multicultural, I believe that each one of them is a *pocket of the promise* of the soon-coming realm of God (DeYoung et al.,

2003).[2] The promise is compelling, and working to tear down racial and cultural segregation in America is a moral imperative for the church. The civil rights movement of the twentieth century was launched by congregational leaders; moral conviction and visionary leadership were keys to their success. Even in the face of counterstories in our culture that suggest acceptance of the status quo, congregational leaders can develop and sustain culturally diverse communities that reflect a vision of the peaceable realm. The testimony and witness from stories of leaders on this new religious border can help us all learn to embrace more effectively the diversity in our midst and to teach our congregants to do the same. This book will share those stories and give you some very practical help to plan and execute this prophetic and purposeful work. It will also help you train other leaders in your context; clergy and laity must do this together.

What can we learn from the stories of clergy who are successfully leading multiracial and multicultural congregations? How did they develop as leaders, and what does that teach us about leadership development? What can their stories tell us about the formation of culturally diverse faith communities of our own? Along with the commitment to proclaim the good news, what other capacities do leaders need in order to help congregations live out an ethic of love and welcoming that creates one family of God? Since real leadership means developing other leaders in a system, how do we preach, teach, plan worship, *and* develop leaders along the way? These are the questions this book will address.

These questions took me to several congregations in search of a model. Middle Collegiate Church in Manhattan caught my imagination. It was Easter Sunday morning, and a jazz quintet was playing on the steps outside before I walked in. Once inside, a multiracial staff in red silk robes greeted me with warmth; several laypeople greeted me as well. The people were spectacular in their diversity; they truly represented the reign of God. There were senior citizens and children; blacks, whites, Asians, and Latinos; couples and families of all configurations, including interfaith couples. The music was outstanding! And there was dance and puppets! The pastor, Gordon Dragt, had agreed to let me study him and his congregation. How did this middle-aged white guy from Michigan hold together such diversity? How did people feel so welcomed, and what made them stay? Gordon and Middle Church, along with four other leaders and their congregations, let me study their stories for my doctoral work; in this book, you will study them as well. I will share what I learned from the clergy and congregations in my study, from my consulting practice at the Alban Institute, and from reading for this project. I will also share what I am now putting into practice in my ministry.

One of the things I learned is that leaders of multiracial and multicultural congregations seem to have in common some aspects of identity, formed by certain environmental, social, and psychological factors, which make them resistant to the dominant culture's views on openness and diversity. They are able to be empathic, to fully welcome the *other*, to hold together cultural diversity, to manage the conflict and change issues that often accompany difference, and to help others do the same. They celebrate and embody the church's multicultural and multiracial mission. We will spend some time analyzing their identity development because I think there are implications in it for developing the leadership capacities needed in culturally diverse congregations. *Leaders can be taught to lead,* so we will discuss implications for your own leadership, and for other leaders in your context as well.

This is a narrative analysis, with stories and storytelling at the core, because people of faith are people of texts. As such, along with texts from psychology, sociology, congregational development, ethics, leadership studies, and literary criticism, I studied *living texts*—leaders and congregations. I used the interdisciplinary sources above to *exegete,* or make meaning, of the living texts. It was fascinating to find wisdom across disciplines that could be applied to leadership in congregations. I learned so much from this work, and you will too! When you are finished with it, you will have

1. Explored the identity stories of five clergy leaders, along with the development of their ethics and vision for multicultural and multiracial ministries. We will specifically explore the ethics of welcome, conflict, truth telling, border crossing, and social justice. How did these leaders get to be who they are? What can we learn from their journeys in terms of developing leadership in emerging multiracial and multicultural contexts?

2. Explored the leadership capacities necessary for envisioning and sustaining culturally diverse communities and coauthoring the vision with congregants. How have these leaders managed holding together cultural diversity? How have these leaders navigated the cultural borders in their contexts?

3. Created a map to explore your own identity, your awareness of self and other, and your leadership style. How did you get to be you? What gifts and passions do you already have for this work, and what capacities do you need to develop?

4. Explored best practices and received practical tools for prophetic preaching, purposeful teaching and planning, and developing leaders in your context. You will also have explored tools for managing conflict, change, and growth. Wherever you are in the process, what else besides God's power do you need to do now to create your own culturally diverse community?

Before we exegete the stories of these leaders and their congregations, I would like to do a few things. First, I will say more about my core thesis: *people and congregations are formed by stories; leadership can create and sustain multiracial and multicultural congregations by **storying** the vision through prophetic preaching, purposeful teaching, leadership development, and planning.* Second, I will discuss the tensions in the predominant culture; there are *counterstories* that undermine the building of multiracial and multicultural communities. Third, I will tell you about some of the sources that will help us analyze, or *exegete*, the stories of our leaders and their congregations.

LIVING TEXTS: A THESIS

Even though there are many ways to conceptualize identity development, I am working from a frame in which identity is formed by stories received from our culture via our families, our peers, and our history. By stories, I mean the telling, enacting, or embodying of historic and mythical events. Stories make meaning for people; they have a beginning, a middle, and an end.[3]

I believe our identities are formed by stories told to us, about us, and around us. We are *living texts*, formed by multiple, interweaving, competing, and, sometimes, conflicting stories that we receive from our culture via our parents, other adults, our peers, the media, and congregational life. Stories about race, gender, theology, generational differences, sexual orientation, ethnicity, and class work consciously and unconsciously to form our identity. Stories also teach us values, ethics, and meaning. Stories help us know who we are and who we are not; they create boundaries, or *borders*, for us. Identity development can be thought of as the process of refining, editing (*redacting*), and *authoring* one's own story in conversation with others. We find our identity in particular contexts—home, school, the marketplace, or church, to name a few. We can think of each of those contexts as a *holding environment*. Whereas the first holding environment is the mother's womb, we continue to develop in holding environments all along our adolescence and throughout adulthood. Individual and group identities are formed in holding environments, or *containers*.[4]

Congregational leaders help form and re-form identity with the stories they rehearse about the peaceable realm of God. Using sacred texts and other texts as sources, leaders weave together congregants' stories, cultural stories, and the story of God's relationship with humanity to answer existential questions and make meaning of life. Paraphrasing Fosters Brooks (*The Expository Times*, vol. 74, no. 9 [1963]: 257–60), leaders preach, teach, and train leaders through their personalities; they *story* the vision through their own living texts. Leaders are *griots*—storytellers who preach, teach, and train leaders through their own complex identity stories.

I am suggesting that, as we study the living texts of leaders of multiracial and multicultural congregations, we find they have some identity traits, or *storylines*, in common. Discovering how they came to be has implications for how to train other leaders because development is an ongoing process. We will also discover core competencies required on multiracial and multicultural borders and how to develop those in ourselves and in others.

In upcoming chapters, we will discuss those storylines the study leaders have in common. We will also discuss how leaders on the border need to narrate the good news in more than one cultural language, verbal and symbolic. They need to be *multivocal* and develop a congregational identity in which cultural diversity is a moral imperative.

Let me pause here to say that although I am interested in the ways the overlapping storylines of race and ethnicity, gender, class, and theology and ethics (*theo-ethics*) form the identity development of leaders, I decided to focus on racial/ethnic and theo-ethical identity for this study because (1) one cannot talk about multiracial churches without talking about race and (2) the theology and ethics of leaders in congregations are at the core of this work.[5]

RACE IN AMERICA: A COUNTERSTORY

Christian biblical images of the peaceable realm are abundant: Isaiah's prophecy of a time when lions will lie down with lambs; Paul's teachings on the equality of male and female, Jew and Gentile, and slave and free; and John's challenge to love the neighbor whom we can see as an expression of the love of God whom we cannot see all echo the gospel teachings of Jesus. Love is the ethic of Jesus of Nazareth—love of God, neighbor, and self. Jesus, Paul of Tarsus told us, is our peace, the one whose love breaks down walls of hostility that separate people. The church, as the Body of Christ, is called and commissioned to break down those walls wherever we encounter them. It is our mission, and we understand that.

Thus, every Sunday morning in American churches, bulletins, greeters, and signs on the door offer messages of welcome. Yet what is often meant by welcome is that strangers can come in as long as they look like us, don't offend us, don't challenge us, and work heroically to fit in with our communal sense of self. In American culture, what we are likely to be made uncomfortable by are racial and ethnic differences, generational differences, theological differences, or differences due to sexual orientation. But, as psychologist Robert Carter argues, what matters most in American culture is race (Carter, 1995).

Though American congregations share the call to welcome, in fact only 7.5 percent of the over three hundred thousand Christian congregations in the United States are multiracial and multicultural, which means no one racial or ethnic group makes up more than 80 percent of its members (DeYoung, Emerson, Yancey, and Kim, 2003). Even churches with a sincere desire to diversify may encounter barriers, such as location, language, and worship style. Dr. Martin Luther King, Jr.'s observation that eleven o'clock on Sunday mornings is the most segregated hour in America still stands to challenge each congregation to examine the difference in its midst and to develop a higher capacity and moral compass to embrace it and to celebrate it.

The gospel message is clear, yet relatively few clergy are able to lead their congregants into this vision of shalom. Clergy do not lead in a vacuum; they work in a context and in a culture that is often counter to the gospel. In other words, the vision we are called to story is often met with resistance that needs to be navigated. We must learn to cross cultural borders and break down resistance to a radical ethic of welcome.

Before we can understand how clergy leaders can tell compelling stories that break down the walls that divide God's people, we must first understand that the identity stories of leaders *and* congregants are formed and re-formed in the context of larger stories, or metanarratives. One such story, for example, is the broader story of the American cultural landscape and, specifically, the cultural issues that affect American religion.

The Story of American Culture and Congregations

America's story is shaped by the stories of many peoples: some born here, some who were forced here, some who chose to come here in search of land, and a place to thrive, some forced off the land that was "discovered." Most of America's peoples, it might be said, yearn for the story that has been called the American dream. That story promises equality to a broad diversity of races and ethnicities and accommodates differences in physical and mental ability, gender and sexual orientations, religions and beliefs. That story promises the right to life, liberty, and the pursuit of happiness. That story promises freedom to live, work, learn, play, and grow where one chooses. That story promises that each of us can worship the God of our choice, in the way that we choose, or to choose not to believe in God at all.

America's history details the tensions between the dream story and reality. In short, the experiment that is cultural diversity in American life is riddled with difficulties. Whether one thinks of America as a melting pot, a salad, a mosaic, or a stew, many communities are still quite racially and economically segregated. Discrimination rears its ugly head in the form of hiring practices and hate crimes. Tolerance for the faith practices of others is sometimes strained at best, and when it is pushed too far, intolerance erupts in defaced synagogues, hate crimes directed toward Muslims, and burned-down churches.

Our country's increasing diversity adds more complexity to the story of how we will live together in the future. As Diana Eck (2001) points out, today the percentage of foreign-born Americans is greater than ever before, even during the peak of immigration a century ago. By most United States census projections, somewhere between 2030 and 2050, visible racial and ethnic minority groups will surpass the population of whites in America, due to immigration patterns and differential birthrates (U.S. Census Bureau, 1992; Sue and Sue, 1999). In the last decade of the twentieth century, the Hispanic population grew 38.8 percent and has surpassed the African American population. In the same time period, the Asian population grew 43 percent (Eck, 2001). In terms of religious diversity, research from Eck's *Pluralism Project* reveals that in America today, there are about six million Muslim Americans, equal to the number of Jews, but greater than the number of either Episcopalians or Presbyterians. Each year, some twenty thousand Americans convert to Islam, and in this post–September 11, 2001 world, hate crimes against Muslims are on the rise as well. The browning of America, the shrinking of the distance between America and the rest of the world, and ever increasing tensions among Christians with differing theologies strain race, ethnic, and faith group relations in our country. Those strained relations affect all of our identity stories.

America's history and present story offer evidence of both failure and moderate success in living with difference. Schools, neighborhoods, and faith communities work hard at this issue. Yet there are tensions. Church growth literature historically suggested that churches grow best in homogeneous contexts. Donald McGavran, based on his thirty years of missionary work in India, created the Institute of Church Growth at Northwest Christian College in Eugene, Oregon, and then moved it to Fuller Theological Seminary in Pasadena, California. McGavran and his successor, C. Peter Wagner, proposed that congregations must be built from homogeneous groups of people. Movement adherents suggest that a higher rate of conversion growth can be predicted for the homogeneous church; it is important that people can "feel at home" and know that they are among "our kind of people." The movement sought to rebut the work of Jürgen Moltmann, for instance, who argues in his *Religion, Revolution, and the Future* that the church, to be authentic, must be heterogeneous, reconciling the educated and the uneducated, black and white, high and low. Moltmann sees the church at its best when it contradicts the natural groupings of human beings, whereas Wagner sees the church as at its best when it conforms to such groupings.

Besides the church growth argument, leaders in many denominations argue that Sunday morning might best be a safe place for restoration and recovery from the stresses of a multicultural week, especially for visible racial and ethnic groups and for recent immigrants who experience oppression in our culture. Still others argue that monocultural churches are important in order to maintain the "root" culture of the so-called white church and the so-called black church (DeYoung, et al., 2003).

Despite these arguments, even if one assumes that many congregations feel called to be diverse, statistics bear witness to the incredible challenge they face. Of the 7.5 percent of the congregations that are multiracial and multicultural, about half of those are in transition due to shifting demographics; only half are intentional about cultural diversity. Catholic congregations are more multicultural than Protestant, and non-Christian congregations are more multiracial and multi-cultural than Christian ones (DeYoung, et al., 2003).

Theologian Howard Thurman, copastor of the Church of All Nations in San Francisco, wondered if the church was "sufficiently religious" or "open [enough] to the Spirit of the Living God" to do the work of breaking down cultural barriers. I think many congregations have the commitment, are open to the Spirit, yet need to develop leadership capacities for embracing and managing cultural diversity. That is my hope, and developing those capacities is the purpose of this book.

THE LIVING TEXTS IN THE STUDY

This book examines the living texts of five particular leaders and their congregations in order to learn from them how we can develop capacities to move into God's future. These leaders share their stories—their testimonies—so that we can learn from their ministries. The congregations in this study are multiracial and multicultural, which means that at least 20 percent of those worshiping differ from the congregation's dominant racial and ethnic group. They affiliate with one of the mainline denominations and are located on the East Coast. They range from pastor-sized to corporate-sized congregations, worshiping with sixty-five to four hundred members on any given Sunday. Middle Church, our model, had 550 members at the time of this study and was worshiping with 350. Each congregation's intentional vision for diversity has been in place for more than three years. The clergy in the study are diverse in terms of race, gender, and age. They include a Puerto Rican born in America, two European Americans, a Korean American, and an African American. There are three men and two women in the study. Their ages range from early forties to early sixties. They are very much like you and me.

Karen Sue Hernandez-Granzen is a Newyorican (Puerto Rican born in New York) Presbyterian clergyperson who has been the pastor of the Westminster Presbyterian Church in Trenton, New Jersey, for nine years. Karen is very proud of her multiracial heritage. She often tells the story of the richness of her Taino Indian, Spanish European, and African bloodlines. These multiple storylines shape Karen's vision for her multiracial and multicultural congregation in which whites, Africans, African-Americans, and Hispanics work and worship together.

About 125 people belong to Westminster Presbyterian Church, and about sixty-five participate in worship there each Sunday. Small in number but rich in spirit, Westminster focuses its ministry on neighborhood children and youth. Get S.E.T. tutoring and mentoring program and

Trenton Youth Connection are just two of the ways West-minster connects with the surrounding community and ministers to the families in the congregation.

Randolph Cassells Charles, a white man who considers himself "ethnically Southern," has been the pastor of Epiphany Episcopal Church in Washington DC for the past nine years. Born in 1947 to a physician and his wife, a former teacher, Randolph grew up in Bennettsville, South Carolina. He lived a relatively privileged life, went to largely segregated schools, and had very little opportunity as a young person to encounter people of other races. As a young man, folk music introduced him to the facts of injustice in the world. The theme of rebuilding and restoring began to emerge in Randolph's life and in his ministry.

Epiphany, in downtown Washington DC, is a community of communities. Some 150–175 homeless men, women, and children worship in the church at eight o'clock in the morning on Sundays. At eleven o'clock, a culturally diverse group of some 150 Episcopalians from the Washington DC metro area gather for worship. During the week, neighbors who work in the local area come to mass. Randolph helps create a community in which racial and ethnic, cultural, and class differences are woven together.

Jong Woo Park has been the pastor of Fairhaven United Methodist Church in Gaithersburg, Maryland, for three years. J.W., as he is called, is a Korean man who was born in Seoul, Korea; he attended college there and seminary in Washington DC. J.W. is the only member of his family of origin in the United States. His father is a retired, high-ranking cabinet member in the Korean government. J.W.'s call to ministry is a fascinating journey across class and geographical borders. Assigned by his bishop to this congregation, J.W.'s challenge is to create a holding environment for a community that is largely African American and white.

Fairhaven is the product of a merger in the 1960s. A Southern Methodist congregation, a Northern Methodist congregation, and a black Methodist church were woven together, they say, into one cloth. Some 120 people gather for worship each Sunday in two services, which blend traditions from the black church and mainline Methodist traditions.

Adrienne Brewington, an African American woman, has been the pastor of Westbury United Methodist Church in Westbury, New York, for three years. A graduate of New Brunswick Theological Seminary, Adrienne served the church for two years before she was ordained this year. She is the first woman and the first African American to serve this congregation. Adrienne is a former actress and gave up a successful law career when called to ministry. She testifies to the fact that miracles still happen.

The Westbury community has been biracial since the Quakers living there freed their slaves in the nineteenth century. Laypeople and leaders are committed to a vision of a racially and culturally diverse congregation; 150 or so people share in worship each Sunday. Although Adrienne's leadership was resisted by some initially, her deep spiritual resources make most say she is "the best thing that has ever happened to us."

Gordon Dragt, a sixty-three-year-old white man, was the pastor of Middle Collegiate Church for twenty years, from 1985 to 2005. Born and raised in Michigan, Gordon graduated from Western Seminary in Holland, Michigan, and served several congregations before coming to Middle Church. Deeply influenced by the life of the Reverend Dr. Martin Luther King, Jr., Gordon's radical ethic of welcome, and the use of the arts in ministry, led to the revitalization and phenomenal growth of his church.

Middle, the model church for this study, is diverse in race, ethnicity, class, gender, theology, and sexual orientation. Members come from the historically artistic East Village, where Middle is located, and from all the Boroughs of New York, New Jersey, and Connecticut. Gordon's ministry of welcome was compelling, so much so that after I completed my research, I accepted a call to serve on staff in January 2004. In July 2005, I succeeded Gordon as Senior Minister.

THEORIES AS SOURCES FOR EXEGESIS

Along with the living texts, theories from other disciplines have much to teach us about *leading on the border*. Two of those sources are the work of theologians: Howard Thurman and Virgilio Elizondo, both border people themselves. Two sources are psychological: Donald W. Winnicott helps us think about holding environments; Howard Gardner helps us theorize about the stories leaders tell.

Howard Thurman and a Theo-ethics of Love

The story, ministry, and writings of theologian and ethicist Howard Thurman are an inspiration to me. His copastorate at the Church for the Fellowship of All Peoples was a model of multicultural and multiracial ministry, one grounded in Thurman's theo-ethical commitment that racial reconciliation is a moral and spiritual issue, one for which each Christian must take personal responsibility. For Thurman, "The walls that divide must be demolished. They must be cast down, destroyed, uprooted. This is beyond debate" (1965, p. 91).

I agree with Thurman that the gospel demands an ethic of love, which manifests itself in authentic, transparent relationships. Thurman's story and his clear articulation of what the ethics of the gospel demand with regard to the human community give us tools for understanding the stories in our study. Thurman will begin to help us ask questions about the theo-ethics of our leaders: What sustains them as they work in culturally diverse communities? What are their theo-ethics of *welcome, conflict, navigating borders, truth telling, and social justice?*

Virgilio Elizondo and a Call to the Border

Mexican American theologian Virgilio Elizondo, a Roman Catholic priest and professor of theology, reminds us that this conversation is not just black and white. His sociological and theological reflections on the *mestizaje*, or mixed-race, nature of both Mexican Americans and the historical Jesus is helpful to us as we consider how living and working where cultures intersect affects storied selves (Elizondo, 2000).

Not only does Elizondo argue that Jesus was mixed race, he reminds us that Jesus' life in Nazareth of Galilee meant constant border crossing; this made Jesus, culturally and linguistically, a *mestizo*, "assuming unto himself the great traditions that flourished in his home territory" (Elizondo, 2000, p. 79). All kinds of people passed through this border town occupied by Roman soldiers. Encountering other cultures shaped Jesus' identity, making Jesus, like Elizondo and our study leaders, a border person.[6]

The gospels tell stories of Jesus crossing cultic borders as well. His table fellowship was scandalous; he broke bread with sinners and tax collectors. He spoke to the unspeakable; he touched the untouchable.[7] On the border, Jesus challenged the cultic status quo. We will learn from our study leaders the impact of crossing borders in multiracial and multicultural contexts. It is part of the *border*, or *mestizo*, identity; those on the border are *multivocal*. Elizondo's story and theo-ethics help us theorize about what leadership capacities are learned on the border.

Elizondo and Thurman remind us of the hope of the gospel story, a story that demands a theological, ethical examination of our community's stories in terms of cultural diversity. Psychological tools also help in this study, as we think of how leaders became who they are. The theories of Donald W. Winnicott and Howard Gardner offer two interpretive lenses through which to exegete the developmental stories of the leaders, to understand the congregational story, and to analyze the dynamic between the leader and the congregation.

Donald Winnicott and Good Enough Holding

As a psychologist from the school of object relations, in which the focus of study is early care, Donald W. Winnicott brings to this study a story of human development that will, among other things, enable us to make compelling connections between the holding environment, or container, of early childhood; the holding environment leaders need to create in order to build authentic communities; and culture itself as a holding environment.

What Winnicott calls "good enough mothering" sets the stage for healthy development in a number of ways, but the idea of *holding* is important for this book.[8] For example, a mother creates a *holding environment* for the child as she cradles him in her arms and creates a safe place for the child to grow. This holding environment is increased with time and space; it becomes a cradle, a playpen, the next room, and eventually the weekly phone call between a parent and an adult child. Thus, the arms-around feeling of the holding environment becomes the *transitional space* in which the child develops; transitional space is also the space for adult living, learning, and playing. It is the space in which art, creativity, and religious experience occur. The concepts of holding and transitional space—*borderspace*—are concepts we will revisit as we think about congregational development and the development of leaders.[9]

Howard Gardner: The Stories Leaders Tell

Howard Gardner, professor of cognition and education at Harvard, may be best known for his theory of multiple intelligences, a critique of the notion of a single intelligence that can be measured by standard psychometric instruments. Gardner, both a developmental psychologist and a neuropsychologist, has focused his work on leadership on the stories leaders tell (1995). His work helps us make connections between a narrative understanding of identity development and the stories leaders tell that form and re-form identity.

In a study of eleven leaders in his book *Leading Minds* (1995), Gardner argues that the "ultimate impact of the leader depends most significantly on the particular story that he or she relates or embodies and the receptions to that story on the part of audiences (or collaborators or followers)" (1995, p. 14). Gardner says further that the stories told are not headlines or snapshots, but "an unfolding drama in which they—leader and followers—are the principle characters or heroes" (1995, p. 14).

I say it this way: Leaders story a vision that revises the stories already existing in the minds of others, and the most compelling stories are the ones that have to do with personal and group identity. The content of the stories leaders tell originates in their childhood experiences; the stories address the ongoing existential concerns over the life cycle. Most important for our work, *effective leaders succeed in conveying a new version of a group's story that makes sense in terms of both where they have been and where they are going. This is a critical competency for leading change.*

Gardner helps us understand that stories about the self and the group convey values and meaning; stories compete with and contradict one another, and familiar stories are more easily assimilated than unfamiliar ones; people resist new stories. Gardner and I agree that stories are best told multivocally—in a way that culturally diverse groups can hear them.

Now that we have had a brief introduction to the leaders in our study, and to some of the theories that will help us exegete their stories, we can more deeply exegete the living texts with the theory, and see what we can learn for our contexts.

CHAPTER 2

STORYING AN ETHIC OF TRUTH TELLING AND SOCIAL JUSTICE

LEARNING FROM LEADERS

INTRODUCTION

As we discussed in the first chapter, I believe people are formed by stories. We are *living texts* formed by multiple, interweaving stories that we receive from multiple sources in our culture. We develop our identity (*find our narrative voice*) in particular holding environments—home, school, the marketplace, or church, to name a few.[1] Individual and group living texts are formed in holding environments. Exegeting the living texts of the leaders in our study will teach us about our own leadership on the border.

This chapter examines the living texts of Karen Hernandez-Granzen and Randolph Cassells Charles. In order to do that, we will use the theories of psychologist Donald W. Winnicott, theologian Virgilio Elizondo, to which we have been briefly introduced, and sociologist W. E. B. DuBois (1903). We will also discuss how our exegesis helps us think about leadership and the theo-ethics of truth telling and social justice.

THE DEVELOPMENTAL STORIES OF LEADERS

Karen Hernandez-Granzen

Karisu, as she was called, is the tenth of eleven children born to a Pentecostal pastor, Jose Belen, and his wife, Margarita. Karen grew up on Staten Island and in Brooklyn, New York. Karen remembers sitting on her mother's knee before her younger brother was born. "She told me I was no longer going to be the baby. I think that made me grow up fast." Karen was always very mature for her age and believes that her mother found that threatening. "She felt I did not need her." In fact, Karen took in the message her mother sent—she *introjected* it. In response, Karen sent back, or *projected*, "I don't need you," in order to survive. Because Margarita prematurely withdrew from Karen, Karen became preoccupied with mom. One of her foundational storylines from Margarita was, "you cannot need me, because I am no longer here."

Karen's father, Jose Belen, was 41 when she was born and her mother was 29. Before marrying Margarita, Jose had been though a period of severe addiction. Then he had what Karen calls "a transformative experience of God," and recovered. One day, working in the family sugarcane fields in Puerto Rico, Jose Belen went up the mountain like Moses; he came down having heard a call to ministry. Jose moved his family to New York. Karen's own story reflects her father's. Almost at the exact time she was experimenting with drugs as a teen, she had a spiritual experience that led her to return to the church fold to serve God passionately.

Karen describes herself as a lonely youth, even in such a large family, with low self-esteem. Some of this can be traced to experiences in school in which her African American and Italian classmates were in tension. Isolated by the fact that she was neither, Karen was also conscious and proud of her own mixed heritage—African, Taino Indian, and white Spaniard.

Along with feeling lonely, Karen had a growing sense of power, about which she was afraid. "I felt people gravitating toward me and being influenced by me, and I feared the power, and the sense that when I spoke, people listened," she shared.

Karen had ambivalent experiences of her father. On the one hand, she has a memory of a fun dad, who took her and her siblings to the park and to music class. On the other hand, Jose was a strict, impatient disciplinarian. "If one [sibling] did something wrong, they would all pay." One of Karen's earliest memories is as a three-year-old. She was in a crib in the nursery, across from her father's office in the church, Iglesia Pentecostal Emanuel, in Brooklyn. "Even though I was alone, I did not cry; I felt safe." Jose Belen, or perhaps the church itself, created a holding environment, which made Karen feel safe. As she matured and followed her own call to ministry, the memory of her father continued to make her feel safe, and then help her see herself in him. "People say I am like my father, who was a man of God." All along the way, other male mentors have substituted for Jose, whose earliest holding helped Karen accept her call to ministry.

Karen also has ambivalent feelings about her mother. Margarita's love meant keeping busy cooking and cleaning; it did not mean spending quality time talking and being with Karen. Karen felt both loved and abandoned. When Jose died, Karen's mom was deeply depressed; essentially both of Karen's parents were gone. Karen shared that her association with "God as father" became very strong. Her God-image and her soul were "healed" as she found a more feminine God in seminary. God has replaced both absent father and absent mother.

One way to interpret this part of Karen's story is that the loss of her father and her mother may have imposed on Karen's growing self. I would call them *impingements* on Karen's growing self, causing her to be more concerned about the moods of others, rather than her own needs. We can recognize what I mean when we think about how many children from alcoholic families have that *walking-on-*

eggshells feeling. They are prematurely concerned about how the system is faring, when they should be appropriately self-concerned. The fact that Karen's parents were absent made her *other-conscious* at an early age. What gifts does other-consciousness bring to leadership on the border, and can we teach that? We will explore those questions toward the end of this chapter.

Randolph Cassells Charles

Randolph Cassells Charles was born in 1947 in Florence, South Carolina, to a physician, Randolph Sr., now deceased, and his wife, Harriet Breeden Charles, who had been a teacher before they married. Randolph experienced his father with ambiguity, describing him as largely absent, but quiet and loving. Even though he was a busy physician, "dad resurrected a Boy Scout troop when I was ready to join, so he could be with us. I felt loved by him in a strange way." Randolph's mother was "present, but cautious," and had high standards. She taught Randolph the value of being "an outgoing Southern gentleman" from a "good family." So, like Karen, Randolph also had ambivalent relationships with his parents.

When Randolph talks of early relationships, Retha, his family's black maid, features prominently. Although many white men and women in the South were cared for by black help, there was something, I believe, unusual if not unique about Randolph's relationship with Retha. It was Retha who held him; it was Retha's arms that were a safe place to rest. In a very frightening storm, Retha rescued Randolph and his brother, Winston, taking them into a closet until the storm passed over. Given Randolph's absent loving father and his present but cautious mother, Retha's holding was formative to Randolph's identity.

Randolph's family life was significantly changed by three deaths that happened in 1957, when he was ten. His aunt and uncle (husband and wife) and grandfather died that year. About his grandfather's death, Randolph said, "I could not stop crying." He went into his father's bathroom (the water closet) and wept by himself, seeking neither parent for comfort. I find it interesting that after the experience of Retha and the storm, being in the water closet without parents was a safe place for Randolph; maybe it was an environment in which he felt *held*. How did absent parents and being held by a black *other mother* inform Randolph's theo-ethics? Even though most of us may not have had those particular experiences, what can we extrapolate from close relationships with the *other* as we study leadership on the border? We will explore those questions after more conversation with our sources.

THE ORIGINS OF THE LIVING TEXT: RELATIONSHIPS

Object Relations Theory

Sigmund Freud's drive theory of development has been revised by the various psychoanalytical schools. One revision is from the object relations school, which makes a shift from Freud's primary focus on the father to a focus on personality development in relationship to the first caregiver(s).[2] An object is a person, place, or thing (or a memory or fantasy of the same) invested with emotional energy. We interact with objects, then, all of our lives; they continue to build our selves and can be either destructive or reparative. These objects might be primary caregivers, siblings, and friends, memories of ancestors, or religious experiences. They might also be messages from the culture about race, ethnicity, and gender or images in the media—embedded in stories.

Narrative Psychology

In another revision of Freud, a narrative psychology perspective considers the self as a set of narrative storylines each person follows in trying to develop an emotionally coherent account of his or her life among people (Schafer, 1994, p. 34). Each person organizes past and present experiences narratively. Rather than conceptualizing the personality as multiple selves (for example, a true, false, or grandiose self), narrative psychologists find it more helpful to conceptualize one person with many storylines that make meaning of his or her life (Schafer, 1992, p. 34).

This is what I mean when I say that identity development can be described as the discovery of one's own narrative voice(s). Identity development, all along the life cycle, is the process of editing, screening and redacting our developmental stories into a cohesive narrative. Each person is the narrator of their experiences with objects that formed their storied selves.

BORDERSPACE, GOOD ENOUGH CARE, AND MIRRORING

Borderspace

D. W. Winnicott is famous for his book *Playing in Reality* (1965), in which he argued that experiences between an infant and caregiver are both subjective (created), objective (real) and on the border. They take place in what Winnicott calls *transitional space*. For example, when a baby sucks a pacifier, it is *both* really a pacifier *and* also a created experience of nursing. It is *both* subjectively a breast *and* objectively a pacifier; it is also on the *border* of each. Whereas Winnicott begins to conceptualize transitional space (*borderspace*) in relation to infant development, we will see that there are implications all along the life cycle. For example, when I think about leadership, I make a connection between *borderspace* and Barry Johnson's concept of polarities. Johnson says that whereas problems can be solved and conflicts can be resolved, polarities must be managed. A polarity means something that is held in tension; it is characterized by *both/and*. The infant's pacifier is both objective and subjective. A person can be both Afrocentric and celebrative of diversity in her or his cultural preferences. We will see that the leaders in the study have the capacity to manage polarities. They have higher tolerance for holding ambiguities. Polarity management is an essential capacity for leading on the border; leaders must be able to manage the *both/and* quality of their ministries.

Central to Winnicott's theory is the concept of *good enough care*. *Good enough care* is what Winnicott means when he describes the ways most parents give themselves over to their infant without resentment. Good enough care enables human development to take place; it makes humanity's inherited potential possible (Winnicott, 1986, p. 145). Good enough care describes the quality of the way a child is *handled* (touched, soothed, rocked), *held* (in the womb, in the arms, and in a safe place), and *presented with objects* the child needs. It also describes the way a child has reflected back a sense of who he or she is, which we call *mirroring*. Handling, holding, object presenting, and mirroring are four critical aspects of good enough care. Good enough care helps create in the growing child a sense of trust, or *belief in*. *Belief in* can be the basis of faith; the way we are held helps us understand the concept of "everlasting arms" (Winnicott, 1986, p. 149). *Maybe good enough care is love.*

For the purposes of this project, the two aspects of good enough care on which we will focus most are holding and mirroring. Holding expands from the womb, to a parent's arms, from dancing on grandfather's feet to baking in the kitchen with friends, from studying in the cafeteria to a weekly phone call to parents. We will talk more about the holding environment in chapter 3, but first I want to talk about mirroring.

Mirroring and the Development of Other-consciousness

We have all experienced how an infant lights up at the smiling face of an adult; psychologists call that *mirroring*. Mirroring means reflecting back to the developing person who they are. It first happens in the mother's face.[3] A mother's wide smile and dancing eyes convey delight in response to the delight she finds in the infant, reflecting who the infant is. The infant sees mommy and sees himself or herself. When care is good enough, children's families give them permission to see themselves in their faces, without evaluation or pressure to change. The child is seen, the child is recognized; the child is understood to be a true self, in the gaze of the ones who care for him or her. As with the Zulu custom of *Imbuntu*, when a child is acknowledged or seen, the child exists. The child grows to be an "I" and gathers information about himself or herself from the "not me" environment. In a good enough context, the developing person introjects goodness and capacity from those he or she idealizes. The child introjects other data, both critical and affirming, from peers and mentors.

If the first face is not a mirror because the caregiver cannot fully be one for the child, the child is imposed upon. *Impinged* by the parent's preoccupation, the child becomes focused on the parent rather than on the self. The child begins to read the caregiver's face and the environment like a map, to see if it is safe to be real. The impingements feel like something to manage. In order to survive, the child develops a compliant self that focuses outward to the gaze of the other.[4] The child becomes *other-conscious*.

In that case, the child's more real self is hidden by this other-consciousness, which protects him or her with compromise, attunement to the other's gaze, and social grace. Most of us have the right dose of this consciousness. It is called manners, or appropriate behavior. When early care has been either extremely deficient or overbearing, there can sometimes be an extreme adaptation in which the real self is fully split off, leaving a false self that is fully compliant, unreal, and dead inside.

For our purposes, I am thinking about the ways some of our study leaders developed a sense of *other-consciousness* in response to their holding environments. One storyline in some of their living texts is an *internalized other voice*, which brings with it some capacities for leading on the border. What are those capacities, and how can other leaders develop them?[5]

Winnicott's Theory as an Exegetical Tool: A Summary

In summary, our earliest caregivers ideally hold us in a good enough environment. As the first mirrors, they may send messages that we are wonderful and whole, or that we must be preoccupied with their preoccupation. When pre-occupied with the gaze of the other, persons introject that gaze as the voice of the *internalized other*. This is what W. E. B. DuBois calls *double-consciousness, or two-ness*.

Second, the relationship between the caregiver and the infant takes place in a borderspace that is both subjective and objective. It is also on the border. This borderspace expands through our life and becomes the space for play, creativity, art, and religious experiences. Multiracial and multicultural environments are borderspace, in which managing polarities and holding ambiguity are key capacities. There is a both/and quality to borderspace. Our study leaders, too, exhibit a both/and quality in their living texts. Winnicott helped us think about other-consciousness; W. E. B. DuBois will help us think about double-consciousness.

W. E. B. DUBOIS AND DOUBLE-CONSCIOUSNESS

Winnicott's theory offers a way to think about experiences that are both subjective and objective, "both/and." In an analysis that predates Winnicott, W. E. B. DuBois suggested that racism in America led to a two-ness in blacks. I have found his analysis helpful for this study of the development of leaders.

The Veil and Double-consciousness

William Edward Burghardt DuBois addressed the issue of the color line in America in a seminal collection of essays, *The Souls of Black Folk* (1903). In the first essay, "Of Our Spiritual Strivings," DuBois introduces the concept of *double-consciousness*, by relating an episode in which the shadow of racism crept across him. As a schoolboy exchanging visiting cards with classmates, he encountered rejection from a new girl at school. With this rejection came a revelation that he was different from the others, shut out from their world with a vast *veil*.

DuBois doubles in his meaning of *the veil* throughout the text. One meaning is the unwarranted and false claims of white superiority that create a wall between blacks and opportunity. Clues to a more positive meaning are found in a reference in black folklore. To be born with a veil, or a *birth sac*, on one's face is to be born with the gift of insight. So the veil has a double, both/and meaning. On the one hand, it is a curse that separates blacks from opportunity, resulting in a double-consciousness, the internalization of a racist gaze. On the other hand, it is also double-sightedness, a gift of perception that can be a survival skill in a racist culture. In our narrative perspective, the veil of racism is a cultural storyline in which white America *writes or projects* onto black America what it means to be black; blacks introject it, to some degree, and then project again what is needed to survive in white culture.

It is important to note that the reality of racism in America means the holding environment is not good enough for *many* of us. It means the mirror of white culture reflects onto many people of color a fractured image, a false image of inherited inferiority. Their souls are impinged. It also means that many whites in America also see a fractured image, one of inherited superiority. Their souls too are impinged. Sociologist Thandeka says that many whites build a self storied in shame because of the dynamics of race in America (Thandeka, 2000). As we will hear when we listen to leaders' stories, all of them are storied by race in America. That counterstory has authored all of our lives, to some degree. It is a story that needs to be revised and transformed.

DuBois and Winnicott, and the Internalized Other Voice

In health, DuBois's meaning of double vision means insight into the culture, language, and mannerism of the other, which enables survival. One has empathy for another, due to mild compliance with the environment. Two-ness enables both/and thinking. It is likely that this kind of two-ness may have origins in holding environments and mirroring that were not quite good enough. When DuBois uses double-consciousness to describe *other-consciousness*, this is clearly synonymous with Winnicott's description of the impinged self; it is more conscious of the needs of others or environmental demands than of one's own inner, true voice. The theories of DuBois and Winnicott converge at the place that I define as the *internalized other voice* (Winnicott called this a *social voice*), which I think makes our leaders able to compromise, be flexible, sense the perspective of the other, and be empathic. With this voice, they can truly *cross borders* to know another. The voice of the internalized other is a fairly healthy adaptation in a complex world.[6] It is formed in experiences of being both accepted and rejected, of belonging to two places, of living on the border. Virgilio Elizondo helps us now look further at border experiences.

VIRGILIO ELIZONDO: PLURAL IDENTITIES ON THE BORDER

Virgilio Elizondo, Catholic priest and theologian, lives in San Antonio, Texas. Elizondo is a self-named Chicano, or a Mexican American, whose basic language and culture is the bilingual, bicultural reality of Tex-Mexicana, *en la frontera* between the Southwest United States and Latin America. Elizondo asserts that he and his people, *la raza mestiza,* are "the first American people, a mixed race people, comprised of the pre-American indigenous people and the European immigrants" (Elizondo, 1983, p. 10). Like Jesus, whom he argues is mixed race also, they have a particular role to play in human history.

The historical Jesus was a Galilean. Galilee was a border town, and those from Galilee had a certain impurity that was cause for rejection (Elizondo, 1983, p. 51). Jesus grew up identifying with the most rejected of society; his love for the rejected ones was both a constraint and a signature of his ministry. Elizondo and others assert that Jesus, who was "culturally and linguistically" a *mestizo*, may have appeared to those of his time to be a biological *mestizo* as well (De Young, 1995).[7] If that is true, then it would follow that Jesus' mixed-race heritage is the means through which God chose to come into the world, creating the opportunity for unity among all the nations. I agree that the very nature of Jesus' mixed-race heritage gave him a special role or calling in the world, one that is shared by *mestizo* people everywhere. Those on the borderspace are inside, outside, and on the border; the borderspace is really a third space in which one is in/out, both/and, and accepted/rejected. It is a place of responsibility and, I believe, power.

Implications for Border Ethics and Mestizo Identity

Jesus' *mestizo* identity has transforming implications for the people of God. First, Jesus offers an opportunity for people to story a new identity and a new family story, with radical love, radical hospitality, and radical forgiveness as core values. Just as Jesus was rejected and then *radically welcomed* (read exalted) by God, so also *mestizo* peoples can move from rejection to that "core liberation that comes only through acceptance, belonging, love, and generosity" (Elizondo, 1983, p. 100). God's love and acceptance of the rejected ones changes them, transforming their experience. Those who have been rejected for their border experiences are accepted as full human beings in the realm of God. Second, I believe the restoried, rejected identity has a deep capacity for empathy and for welcoming others. There is *grace* in the hearts of the ones who once were lost and now are found. Those on the border have the power to transform others through a radical welcome and acceptance.

Ethics on the Border: A Summary

Stories of acceptance and rejection, stories of belonging and being alien, and stories of both intimacy and distance shape a *border theo-ethic* of radical welcome and acceptance.

Border theo-ethics are prophetic ethics, the practice of which re-
quires conversational engagement across cultural borders. I also
believe border ethics require one to be able to tell compelling
stories (offer hope for a preferred reality) in the languages
of both those who accept and those who reject; one needs to
be able to "speak in tongues."[8]
    As races and cultures mix, two things are to be expected.
First, there is conflict and tension, as people learn to live with
difference. Second, old categories cease to be meaningful. In
this case, Elizondo helps illuminate that two categories—
both/and—are not enough. Maybe we need three—both this
and that, and fully neither, in order to name the plurality and
diversity we are facing (Anzaldua, 1987). The leaders in this
study have at least a two-ness, and because of the two-ness,
there is mixing, or *mestizaje*; a third thing is developing. It is
yet unnamed, emerging, and dynamic. Although it is
presently nameless, we might call it a multivocal identity. As
we return our attention to the storied selves of Karen and
Randolph, let's think about the relationship between mirroring and identity development.

On Imperfect Mirrors, Survival, and the Racial-ethnic Storyline

    When we exegete Karen's story, we notice that with the
death of her father, and the depression of her mother, her
mother and father mirrors were gone. In order to adapt and
survive, Karen focused outward for an approving gaze.
Karen has an internalized other voice. It is a gift to her ministry. With it, Karen is able to articulate a border ethic in
which the other is valued, and she is also able to value the
otherness in herself. "I am proud that I am three ethnicities;
I call myself Newyorican to capture the borders on which I
sit." How did that happen?
    Karen spent the first ten years of her life on Staten Island.
She was "a minority among minorities." As part of the only
Puerto Rican family in an Italian community, Karen learned
that even though she was a person of color, she did not experience the same aggressive racism the Italians had toward

blacks; she was not as dark. Further, even though the Italians were ethnic folk, they had more power. Karen was not white, so she experienced racism. She was not black, so she experienced less racism. Karen was both oppressed and privileged.

Karen embodies in her flesh the multiculturality that she feels called to live out. Her ability to cross borders begins with early experiences of acceptance and rejection, of feeling both inside and outside of various boundaries in the church and in the world. She, like Elizondo, has a story formed on borders.

In Winnicott's theory, people who have been impinged continue to fill their experience with impingements, to seek out that which they know. I think that may be true. But, I would add, people who learn how to have border experiences continue to be affirmed for doing so, and they seek those experiences out. Karen's ministry took her to several of those kinds of experiences. She worked in a Spanish-speaking church that was Eurocentric in its worship style. She worked in an historic, large, white, Presbyterian church and helped introduce the congregation to multicultural worship. Both of these experiences helped Karen hold together the "passionate, festive, and spontaneous" gifts of Hispanic worship and the "more solemn, liturgical, and highly intellectual Eurocentric worship." She can lead worship in multiple cultural voices; she is *multivocal*. Karen did border crossing in each of these contexts. Perhaps, like Elizondo, she grew to like the both/and of these experiences.

Like Virgilio Elizondo, Karen has had positive and negative experiences because of her race and ethnicity. Karen had a series of very powerful experiences of affirmation due to her brown skin in her denominational work. At a women's conference, "All of the brown women ... thought I was one of them." Traveling in the Middle East, people everywhere thought she was one of them; her brown skin made that happen.

On the other hand, Karen's "brownness" created a negative experience when she was a student at New York City Technical College. She was chosen to be part of Mobil Oil's

Minority Student Week and worked for them for two summers. A teacher shunned both her brownness and her urban experience, telling her that she "rose to the top of the garbage heap." At the time of this study, at age 42, Karen continued to struggle with the oppression she internalized from *reading* and introjecting the racist storyline (one of the voices she internalized). But she is more comfortable using her gifts. "It surprises me when my internalized racism sabotages me." Recall that I am arguing that identity development means narrating and *redacting* one's own story. As such, Karen continues to claim her gifts and her authority as a pastor, as a woman of God, and as a leader. In a healing dream, Karen claimed her pastoral authority in an all-white context. Dressed in her collar, she claimed her worth. Karen's clerical collar symbolizes the pastoral authority that facilitates bridge building and crossing borders. I believe it also symbolizes the father mirror, who preceded her in ministry. Finally, it symbolizes being held together by the acceptance and love of God, who is both father and mother, and who mirrors to Karen the gifts that being on the border have storied in her.

Thinking about Karen's absent parents, recall that Randolph's father was mostly absent, offering little mirroring. Recall also that his mother's mirror was full of caution and correctness. I believe both impinged young Randolph; he did not get to revel in an anxiety-free mirror. The absent mirrors left Randolph with a voice of the internalized other as well.

Whereas Karen speaks of many border-crossing experiences, Randolph grew up with very few relationships with people of color; he knew Retha, the gardener, and some coworkers at his summer job. In Randolph's family, there was no open hostility toward people of color, nor did they work for racial justice. Randolph called it "polite racism," which for him was just as hostile but a different language.

Randolph learned in his family more about being Southern than about being white. Psychologists of racial identity development say most American whites have no self-conscious racial identity. Because whiteness is not often rejected, it does not become a salient trait. Randolph's whiteness was not an issue for him while he was growing up white, male, Southern, and privileged (Helms, 1990; Tatum, 1997; Perry, 2001). As an adult narrating his own story, Randolph is very conscious of the fact that his privilege is mirrored from many sources. "When I grew up doors were open to me because I am white and middle class. [Now], it might be because I am a person of some power: white, gray, male, heterosexual, middle class, and wearing a collar," he said.

But those are not the only storylines Randolph is narrating. He very much identifies with so-called black culture. His early care, and Retha's mirroring, set the stage for a both/and racial and ethnic identity. I believe also that Randolph's parents held Retha—in high esteem and without disregard—as she held him. In other words, they enabled him to respect her and to take her in as goodness. As Randolph narrates his story, he talks about having an emotional attachment to African American, "mom and pop" establishments, tucked away in the shadows, "with food that tastes like home." Because he is a priest, he is welcomed. It is because of his unique relationship to Retha that he feels at home in the bosom of black America. She was his safe holding environment. His imaginings of a good home were shaped by the one time he saw hers; it was simple, basic, clean, and warm. He became conscious of how other she was: African American and of a different class. He identified with her otherness, maybe due to his own sense of disconnection from his parents. The memories of Retha and her mirroring and holding shape in Randolph a border ethic that makes him want to create multiracial environments and to break down class barriers. Retha forms Randolph's theoethic of social justice.

Although their living texts are very different in terms of racial and ethnic heritage, class, regional ethos, gender, and denominational experience, Randolph and Karen have some things in common as well. Both felt displaced by younger siblings,[9] and experienced deaths of loved ones at an early age; both of their mothers and fathers were absent mirrors in significant ways, and both had early experiences with different cultures that I argue form their racial and ethnic identities. In Randolph's case, Retha was an "other mother" and a black mirror to a growing white child. In Karen's case, the mirror was the false construct of racism in America that sent her a refracted image of her self-worth. Both had early experiences moving across borders. Both felt called to be in ministries where cultures blend, and both came to find that their clerical collars facilitated moving across borders.

Karen and Randolph exhibit evidence of double-consciousness, and I believe the existence of two identities in them leads to a third, hybrid, emerging identity, or *mestizaje*. Karen speaks of her own multicultural identity. Randolph speaks passionately about something developing in him, a transformation happening in him. I would argue that the experiences of being on the border formed these leaders, and it continues to form them. This ongoing border crossing changes them and helps them change the cultures of their congregations. The mixing, or *mestizaje*, enables them to lead multiracial and multicultural churches. Let us now turn to the development of theo-ethics in Karen and Randolph.

IMPLICATIONS FOR LEADERSHIP: THE THEO-ETHICS OF TRUTH TELLING AND SOCIAL JUSTICE

Managing Conflict with the Truth

We have talked about how Karen and Randolph have narrated the storyline of racial and ethnic identity. Recall that identity comprises interweaving and complex storylines that form and reform each other. Border crossing, then, storied not only race and ethnicity, but gender, class, and theology and ethics. Let's focus now on theo-ethics.

Karen's theo-ethics are the products of her identity development; they grow out of making meaning, as she redacts her story. Themes of acceptance and rejection from racism in our culture have joined with loss and grief to give her an internalized other voice, which facilitates empathy and "getting along." Part of "getting along" means compliance. But, for Karen, surviving her life meant showing her true self—telling the truth—to God. There, in the face of her father-and-mother mirror, she could reveal her broken self and be accepted, held, and repaired.

Karen's spirituality rests squarely on confidence that she belongs to God. This feeling stems from losing her father and, essentially, her mother (due to depression) at an early age. Recall that God was the parent on whom she could depend. She remembers, as a teen, "being with my friends and being high, and having clarity that this was just a phase. I was able to state, without a shadow of a doubt, that I was going back to church and to heaven." Living outside of the church, yet inside God's grace, was another example of Karen living on borders. It seems that even though Karen did some things to hide her impinged self with missing parental mirrors, she always knew her true self belonged to God. Telling the truth to God storied in Karen a radical theo-ethic of truth telling, with which she crosses borders in her denomination and in her congregation.

Karen deals with the truth in her ministry by putting herself in the other person's shoes. Empathically, she asks: "How would I want to be told the truth in a situation?" and then she puts that insight into action. Karen believes both in putting issues on the table and having no one shamed by the truth. When it comes to conflict, Karen focuses on the facts. She has no tolerance for gossip or for keeping things pent up inside. Her motto is *no tengo pelo en la lengua*, which means, "I have no hair on my tongue." Karen encourages her congregation to speak the truth in love. She manages conflict in her congregation with open communication, truth telling, patience, and a careful use of power. For Karen, each part of the Body of Christ is important, and speaking the truth honors that, as does understanding how to share our God-given power as the church builds the realm of God.

As I think about Karen as a leader, not only is her theo-ethic of truth telling notable, it is important to this project to hear how Karen stories God. For Karen, God is in every way a fact of life; that is both a challenge and a comfort. God's all around holding filled a void in the absence of a mirror; God is unbounded and present in the insecure times of border crossing. Karen is challenged by the implications of the unbounded nature of God as it relates to servant leadership. She wrestles with the sense that as a servant, she too should be unbounded—in a culture that expects women and people of color to overfunction. Karen wrestles with a servant motif in this context, and with how to claim her power. So the seeming duality of servanthood and power are part of Karen's two-ness as well.

Key to Karen's understanding of the gospel is both that it breaks down walls (crosses borders) and brings unity and that it is to be particularly appropriated in each culture (inside borders). This is another example of two-ness, or both/and thinking.

Making the Crooked Places Straight

Randolph's maid Retha served as an other-mother mirror. Because of this, he continues to feel more at home in African American situations. We might say that he looks in the mirror and sometimes sees a black person there, despite the acceptance his white, middle-class self receives from our culture. The sense of otherness may feel more real (read *true*), because of the distance and lack of mirroring he received from his parents, which lead him to sense his own internalized other voice. The black woman who loved him was poor. Inside himself, Randolph is rich and poor, black and white, and he is on the border. He is *mestizaje* culturally and spiritually and is on the way to some third thing that is yet unnamed. For Randolph, his theo-ethic of social justice has roots in his privilege, which stood apart from Retha's nonprivilege.

After graduation from seminary, Randolph was assigned to two parishes simultaneously: an African American mission, where two former slave chapels had merged, and an all-white parish. Randolph felt more comfortable in the black

31

parish and was deeply influenced by his relationship with the former rector's widow, Miss Ruby, an old, wise, black saint of the church. Randolph served another congregation in Virginia before becoming the rector of Epiphany, where he has been for nine years.

Randolph's ethics of social justice also have roots in the folk music of his youth. He had a friend in ninth grade whose brother had a great sound system and "great music, including Bob Dylan, Peter, Paul and Mary." The young men sang, "The Times, They are a-Changing" at high school graduation; for Randolph it was a moment of rebellion. Through that music, his eyes were opened; it revealed to him, and mirrored to his emerging self, how injustice and racial and economic oppression were affecting the country.

In Randolph's view, race and class intersect to create borders that are difficult for communities to cross. "You can have blacks and whites together of the same class, but getting the smelly poor and the rich together is tougher," he said. In his congregation, they are focusing on race and class issues. In Randolph's theo-ethics, racial justice and economic justice are inextricably connected. The ministries at Epiphany reflect his conjoining of the two, as does his theology.

Randolph's God storyline is not so much about how God relates to the world as how the world relates to God. He is clear that we do not know the whole story. God is always present, loving us and using us to be instruments of God's peace. We relate to God in a variety of ways, which, he says, leads to confusion of boundaries and pluralism, different faith journeys and identities, searching and getting lost. Randolph believes God values our differences and wants the world to live in harmony. Randolph is both particularly Christian and acknowledges many paths to God, a manifestation of his both/and way of being in the world.

A central image in Randolph's core religious beliefs is the reign of God, in which humans live in relation with God, who is creator, power, and source of all life; and in which family means not only a global community but also relating to creatures and the environment. Jesus' incarnation was so that we would learn to live with diversity. In relation to God, Randolph believes, we can move deeper and beyond our skin to other levels of awareness. Randolph summarized, "Through compassion and grace, we can truly identify with another, cross barriers that separate us, and therefore accept ourselves more fully."

CONCLUSION: THEORY EXEGETING STORIES

In this study, I have introduced several theoretical tools by which the living texts of Karen and Randolph were read. The object relations theory of Donald W. Winnicott, the racial analysis of W. E. B. DuBois, and the border ethics of Virgilio Elizondo gave us language with which to look at the racial and ethnic and theo-ethical storylines of our leaders. Further, as we thought about their development, we discovered some implications for leading on the border.

What are we discovering as we exegete the storied selves of the leaders through the theory? The ways these leaders survived rejection and the absence of mirroring led them to be prematurely outwardly focused. As a result, they developed an internalized other voice. That voice is a gift to their ministries. Leaders of multiracial and multicultural congregations have a two-ness, or plural identity, that helps them live with ambiguity. They are good at both/and thinking. They extend welcome, either due to rejection in their lives or profound acceptance by "the other." They walk the walk and talk the talk. Their development also storied in them particular ethics: for Karen the obvious passion is for truth telling, and for Randolph it is social justice.

Not all of us have profoundly missing mirrors in our pasts. Not all of us grew up negotiating race and ethnicity on the border. But most of us have had parenting that was only *almost* good enough, and so have adapted with some kind of internalized other voice. All of us have been storied by race in America. All of us have experienced borders like in/out, win/lose. We have storylines of otherness. How do we access that empathy, that compassion, and the capacities that a *self-conscious awareness of otherness* can bring? I am convinced that developing leaders on the border-spaces means creating border experiences. We can story a multiracial and multicultural world when we rehearse the realm of God in our congregations. To paraphrase psychologist Erik Erikson, culture changes us and we change culture. To create the picture of the preferred reality for which we hope, we need experiences on borders. We need to feel rejected, and then accepted. We then need the opportunity to welcome and accept others. On the border, we develop twoness in our storylines, we become the emerging third *raza*; we are *mestizaje*. On the border, we both hold together our unique particularity and value the unique particularity of the other. There we converse with the other and with the otherness of ourselves. On the border, we are transformed.

Our next chapter affords us the opportunity to exegete the stories of Jong Woo Park and Adrienne Brewington. We will focus on the relationship between the ways they were *held* and the ways they hold their congregations through managing conflict and creating appropriate boundaries.

CHAPTER 3

STORYING AN ETHIC OF CONFLICT AND BORDER CROSSING

LEARNING FROM LEADERS

INTRODUCTION

As we briefly reviewed in chapter 2, good enough care includes the concept of *holding*. Holding denotes not only the actual physical holding of the infant but also the entire environment that facilitates development. Good enough holding is critical for the development of the intellect and the imagination, the use of symbols, and relationships with others. It also enables trust, which helps the developing child have faith in an appropriate belief system. Before I say more about holding, let's begin to hear the stories of Adrienne and Jong Woo.

READING LIVING TEXTS

Adrienne Brewington

Adrienne, an African American, forty-five-year-old woman, has been the pastor of Westbury United Methodist

Church for three years. A graduate of New Brunswick Theological seminary, she was ordained in 2003. She is married to her best friend, Fred, with whom she went to junior high and high school. Her mother fixed them up, and they have been together ever since. Adrienne studied theater in undergraduate school and made her living for a while as a struggling artist. Encouraged by her spouse, she went to law school but left her lucrative law practice when called to go into ministry. Growing up in and out of the church, and not too deeply committed to it, Adrienne describes a profound experience of conversion that led her to ministry. During the time she and her husband were thinking about having children, Adrienne was in great pain. She prayed, "I can't live if you don't help me." In answer to her prayers, "the pain was gone; the room was full of light." Feeling that God was speaking to her, Adrienne went to seminary and entered the ordained ministry.

Adrienne and her two siblings grew up with their mom, a schoolteacher, and their father, a jazz musician. Adrienne's dad gave up his musical career and became a postal worker so he could be home to take care of his children after school and on weekends. The sacrifice her father made is really important to Adrienne; he was quite accomplished and let go of all of that in order to hold his family. This is the same quality of holding Adrienne gets from God, from whom she experiences the love of a radical sacrifice. She says, "Look, if God can die and rise again, God can do anything."

Adrienne's parents grew up in the same community; their mothers were acquaintances. Adrienne's mother encouraged her to excel academically. She gave Adrienne loving, tenacious, and bottomless care. Adrienne said, "Whatever you need, she had it. Mom thought ahead. If I needed a purple crayon, it was in her purse." Basically, if you needed it, when you needed it, Mom would provide it, a good enough quality for sure. Chris also told Adrienne there was nothing she couldn't do. "Mom heard me pretending not to be smart with a boy and told me to never do that again." Even though mother and daughter had a complex relationship, Adrienne's mom was a mirror that reflected back possibility and capability. Adrienne saw in her mother-mirror her truest self.

Despite racial politics in America, Adrienne's mother also passed along a sense of entitlement to all of the good things in life. Adrienne's great-grandmother was an enslaved African who married an octoroon.[1] The children were various shades of brown. Adrienne's own grandmother was lighter brown and was mistreated by her very dark mother. The *colorism* was so severe that a German woman took her grandmother in and raised her in Georgia. Adrienne's maternal grandmother then passed on to her two children a sense that they were deserving of the same privileges as whites. This is a value that was passed on to Adrienne from her mother. In other words, in a world in which race, class, and gender oppress, Adrienne was held in such a way as to convince her of her entitlement to all good things. Adrienne said, "Going to white schools, I had kind of a white aspect. I felt entitled to all the things they were." Adrienne's storyline of justice and reconciliation is formed in this holding environment: all people are entitled to all good things; reconciliation among peoples will help make that happen.

Jong Woo Park

Jong Woo has been the pastor of Fairhaven United Methodist Church since July 2001. Jong Woo, or J.W. as he is called here in America, was born in Seoul, Korea, in 1963. He is the last of five children. He, his brother, and three sisters lived with their mother in the country while their father served first as a major general in the army, then as the vice-secretary of defense.

J.W.'s mother, unlike most of the mothers of the other study leaders, was home and present for her children when he was growing up (recall that Karen's mother was depressed for critical periods of her childhood, Randolph's mother was not present to him in nurturing ways, and Adrienne's mother worked as a teacher). But he, like they, shared ambivalent, or both/and, feelings about her parenting. As J.W. describes her, she was "on the one side strict and on the other side generous." She was strict about being diligent and not wasting resources and generous when it came to her children making mistakes. She was both conservative and full of grace, which are descriptors J.W.'s congregation uses about him.

As a young child, J.W. experienced his father as both militaristic and compassionate. J.W. theorizes that the tension in his father's personality resulted from his own parenting. J.W.'s paternal grandfather was "like an old lady" in a culture that demanded certain strength from men, so perhaps J.W.'s dad overcompensated and joined the army. As time passed, J.W.'s father grew to be really caring and very compassionate. "When I was young, I did not think my father was kind. Later I found that other part of him and loved talking to him."

J.W.'s parents held him in ways that were complex. Militaristic, then kind, his father grew from a remote general to a friend, over time. Compassionate and strict, J.W.'s mother held him with grace that I believe prepared him for being gracious to and in his own congregation. Vestiges of his father's holding environment show up in J.W. in the form of gender types (men don't cry) that are then reformed in his relationship with Hi Rho, his wife. We shall find as we hear more of his story that J.W. is a border crosser: wealthy then poor, Korean then American, Buddhist/Confucian then Christian, stern then soft.

Why are we talking about stories of holding? It is because Adrienne, J.W., and all clergy are "parents" who hold the congregational system and facilitate development. I am suggesting that how they were held stories the ways they hold others. The way you were held affects the way you hold. Let's talk more about holding and then reflect on leadership.

ORIGINS OF THE LIVING TEXTS: THE ENVIRONMENT

Good Enough Holding

Holding, we have discussed, facilitates the steady progress of development all along the life cycle. The parents hold the child when he or she is absolutely dependent, when the child is relatively independent, and when the child is moving towards independence. The child moves toward growth through holding and through an accumulation of memories of holding, which are organized narratively. When all is good enough, the child develops trust in the environment.

The mother first holds the infant in her womb. The father (or someone else) holds her while she holds the child. The culture also holds her, sometimes in ways that are not good enough. The holding environment increases with time and space; it becomes the mother's arms, a cradle, a playpen, and the next room. It can be the safe space in which dad tosses the child into the air, nana's kitchen down south, or dancing on grandpa's feet. It can be a college dorm room or the monthly phone call from overseas. Basically, the concept of holding asserts that the parents have attuned to the evolving needs of their developing child. Holding facilitates relating to objects (recall: persons, places, or things with emotions attached to them), reality testing (sensing what is real and what is subjective), and creative play. The quality of the holding environment is about the behavior of those who hold.

So holding meets both physiological needs and psychological needs. The empathic, good enough caregiver makes the environment reliable; he or she considers the infant's sensitivity to touch, temperature, and sound. The caregiver's good enough holding includes all of the care he or she gives the infant, throughout the day and night. It includes the ways he or she protects the child from his or her own moods (impingements) with good enough boundaries. But it is especially the physical arms-around holding of the baby, in which the parent first demonstrates his or her love.

Illusion, Transitional Phenomena, and Play

As good enough care means adapting to the child, one very important adaptation is to present what the baby needs when he or she needs it. At just the right time, when the bottle or breast is presented, the baby feels magically responsible for making it happen; it is as though the baby creates it. This *illusion* is a very healthy one that helps the child grow. Baby can create the breast over and over again, until the caregiver disillusions the child, at just the right time. Both of these acts of holding—illusion and disillusion—help the baby move toward relating to objects outside of himself or herself.

Not only does the mother present the needed breast, she presents objects with which she and the baby play. A teddy bear comes to represent the relationship with the mother. It smells like her. In play, the baby first finds a bear then creates for himself or herself the comfort of mommy. Through this dynamic of play, the child grows confidence to create the world. Playing (or *illusory experience*) takes place in the space between the mother and the infant. The transitional space is not only an inner reality nor is it just external or shared reality; it is both. It is on the border of objective and subjective, on the border of created and found. The transitional space is a playground on the border of subjective and objective. The subjective/objective objects in potential space like a teddy bear or a pacifier are called transitional objects or phenomena.[2] In the *borderspace,* creativity emerges.

In summary, then, holding and playing experiences are the origins of healthy development. Playing is also the origin of all creativity; science, music, and religious experience have their roots here. Borderspace and play are the essential building blocks of the development of culture. Next, we will explore how these concepts can help us think about how religious experience rehearses the realm of God.

Borderspace and Religious Experience

Beginning in infancy and continuing throughout the life cycle, play, or illusory experience, constitutes the greatest part of experience. Defined the way we have above, play includes symbol usage, creating chalk paintings on the sidewalk, composing or enjoying symphonies, diving into the ocean, and praying or partaking of the Eucharist.[3] Play is universal; it facilitates growth and health, and it enables the formation of group relationships, including congregations. Psychologists of religion help us see that Winnicott's concepts of good enough caring and transitional phenomena have important implications for the study of religious experience.[4] The ability to play; to live creatively; to produce art, literature, and science; and to have religious experiences—all of these take place in borderspace. There is a straight developmental line from playing with mom to playing with friends to cultural experiences. Religious experience is such a cultural experience. Good enough holding enables the individual to experience this line of development and to play. However, failure in holding impinges the ability to play, to have religious experience, to use symbols, and, ultimately, to feel alive.

Psychologist Ann Ulanov writes poetically about a God who "lets himself be eaten like a good mother, receiving our hungry attacks and voracious appetites. We consume this God, who nevertheless survives and remains faithful to us" (Ulanov, 2001, p. 58). The experience of being held by a good enough caregiver who survives the infant's appetite prepares the growing child for relating to God. Much of what we think about God and experience in religion comes from our experience with early caregivers.

Good enough holding facilitates the development of a true self. We can extrapolate from that some learning about religious experience. We can imagine that the experience of "true religion" is real and holds together the good and bad of human experience. It provides a way to manage the both/and nature of life. Rather than increasing the fractures in the spirit, it holds us together; we don't have to split good from bad in order to survive. We understand the both/and nature of life and develop theologies that make sense out of gray: everything is not black and white, we learn. True religion helps us proclaim that, even in the midst of the ambiguities of life, God is with us. However, false religion and a less-than-real self result from impingements. False religion can split spirit and intellect, grace and judgment, personal piety and justice works. It quite quickly implies that some people are all bad and that some others are all good. It has less tolerance for complexity and ambiguity. It cannot hold together the tensions life brings; splitting becomes the defense.

When we split our image of God into the good parent who always comes and also the bad parent who seems elusive and slow to answer our prayers, we are constructing a false god, whom we falsely believe is more manageable. The most helpful religious experiences help us hold together all our experiences of God, even as the good enough parent holds together our many different storylines.

Religious experiences—worship, preaching, rituals, and relating to a faith community—hold identity, familial, cultural, and religious stories. They also hold confidence and hope. For example, preaching holds stories of redemption and transformation.[5] Preaching is one form of storytelling. Preparing for sermons, including exegesis; the preparation of a text, either oral or written; and delivery in the context of worship might all be considered transitional experiences. In those processes, the preacher engages in a form of "play" as he or she stories the vision of a preferred reality. The preacher then invites others to play in that reality as well. In worship, the community is held together as they rehearse the realm of God.

Rituals in worship hold both the transformational experiences of new life in baptism, and those present in sharing the Eucharistic meal with Christ and our communities. They are two of the spaces in which our potential to be all that human beings can be are actualized. The ways these two sacraments are experienced can be traced back to childhood holding. For example, one can ask: How is the experience of being bathed by loving, holding hands a transitional experience that prepares us to receive baptism as a symbol? Certainly, one can argue that the quality of holding and feeding at one's mother's breasts are transitional experiences that inform our experience of the Eucharist. Elements of the liturgy—including hymns, shared readings, patterns of standing or kneeling for prayer—are all enactments of stories and memories, which hold the congregation together.

The space for play and imagination is essential for healthy living. Religious experience allows us to imagine ourselves, and all of creation, in new, more whole ways, and to rehearse that new reality. Leaders in congregations create a holding environment for playing in the realm of God. In chapter 5, we will have some practical conversation about storying the realm of God through preaching, worship, and rituals. Now we discuss the theology of Howard Thurman, who held together one of the first multiracial and multicultural congregations in America. His living text, his theo-ethics, and his exemplary leadership are all important for our study.

HOWARD THURMAN: HOLDING AND THEO-ETHICS

Howard Thurman spent part of his ministry as the co-pastor of the multiracial and multicultural Church for the Fellowship of All People in San Francisco, California, the first multiracial and multicultural congregation in the United States (De Young, Emerson, Yancey, and Chai, 2003, p. 64). As a theologian and ethicist, Thurman's living text invites questions that are pertinent to this study. How was this African American man held such that he wanted to be on the border of race and ethnicity? How did he hold together difference in his context? Let us now exegete his story.

Howard Thurman was born in the segregated town of Daytona, Florida, in 1900. By all accounts, Thurman's mother was a devout Christian who, along with her mother, taught Thurman the importance of spiritual values and compassion for others. Grandma Nancy instilled in Thurman a belief in him that helped him deal with the experiences of racism and segregation in the South. She also instilled in him a thirst for knowledge that helped liberate him from his humble beginnings. Even though Dayton's school district only allowed blacks to finish up to seventh grade, Grandma Nancy insisted that Thurman be allowed to finish eighth grade, and, in the shadow of the deaths of his father and stepfather, managed to scrape up enough money to send young Howard away to Jacksonville to high school.

Thurman's father, Saul, never joined a church. When he was buried, the pastor used him as an object lesson to sinners; he was going to hell because he had never joined the church. Thurman vowed that he would never have anything to do with the church, which rejected his father and later would not let him join.

Despite economic stress and racial segregation, Thurman's grandmother was good enough. Grandma Nancy exercised control over her environment, stressing that the individual was the key to social change. Thurman's grandmother made a difference in his world; she revealed to him the power of love. By doing so, Grandma Nancy facilitated an environment in which Thurman's theo-ethics of love could develop. In other words, part of Thurman's narrative voice (identity) is one that claims the ethic of love as triumphant over hatred and rejection. Thurman's holding environment eventually extended from his grandmother to the spirituality she valued, despite his own negative experiences. Not only did she hold Thurman, he found solace (holding) and a sense of self in prayer and meditation in the woods or along the beach in Florida.

Despite growing up in a racist culture and experiencing rejection and racism in the church, Thurman managed to maintain a belief in community, the power of love, and the way the imagination can allow each human being to relate to and connect with another. Writing in *The Luminous Darkness*, Thurman refers to the leap of the imagination that happens when people are in authentic community. "When this happens, men are free to relate to each other as human beings— good, bad, mean, friendly, prejudiced, altruistic, but human beings. . . . This is the precious work of the imagination."[6] The imagination to which Thurman refers is what we have been calling *play*. Thurman's writings indicate the many experiences that offered him good enough holding: his grandmother's faith in God and in individual effort, the value placed on education in a community influenced by Mary McLeod Bethune, the quiet of the beach, prayer and meditation, the nonviolence teaching of Mohandas Gandhi. These experiences of being well held, one might say, gave Thurman the capacity for great empathy, for great imagination, and for "playing" in that borderspace in which humanity has great love for one another.

Racism, False Boundaries, and Failure in Holding

Recall that holding refers to the entire facilitating environment. When we think of Thurman's story, it is fair to say that racism in America impacted the holding environment. Racism in America creates a holding environment that forces people to have less than authentic selves. In order to survive many people artificially split the "good objects" from "the bad objects."[7] This results in prejudice and racism. Howard Thurman describes a need for care that is so fundamental to life and spiritual health that when it is denied, an inner conflict results. He says, "The conflict expresses itself in many ways, from profound mental disturbance to the complete projection upon others of the hate and violence the person himself is feeling" (Thurman, 1979, p. 170).

Additionally, we can say racism affects not only the holding environment of people of color; it affects the holding environment of all Americans. All Americans are affected by the foul stench of racism on school systems, health care, images in the media, and quality of housing and economic disparity. Racism destroys community, and robs humanity of authentic relating. Segregation, poverty, and racism were all factors in Thurman's upbringing that were somehow transformed by the "holding" of a loving grandmother and a caring immediate community. Thurman, thus held, imaged the Beloved community—all those who share an ethic of love— as the ideal holding environment, or *container*.

Holding, Religious Experience, and the Ethic of Love

What am I saying, then about holding, religious experience, and theo-ethics? If congregations are to be good enough holding environments, their leaders as the ones commissioned to *hold* the beloved community, cannot accept racism, discrimination, segregation, oppression, and separation as by-products of a racist America. They must not only demand that divisive walls of hostility be demolished, they must also insist that damage done by existing walls be repaired as well. Congregational leaders cannot be satisfied until they story for the church that false borders among races, theologies, and even differing faiths must be redefined. When our work is finished, all people who seek God and work on behalf of radical love are included in the family of God. A radical ethic of love becomes the *collective identity* of God's people. It isn't that an individual identity is discounted and merged into a group identity; people do not lose their unique particularities. Rather, they are interrelated and interdependent. In the holding environment of true community, people share experiences of meaning—they share storylines, which are more compelling than the barriers or boundaries that separate them. These common narratives prepare the way for reconciliation. Leaders on the border know that communities are held together by love and mutual respect for the particularity of the other. Three of the leadership capacities they require are the ability to (1) help people tell their stories, (2) help people listen to the stories of others, and (3) weave those stories together.

Loving one another across boundaries requires some element of risk and vulnerability. It also requires some sense of feeling grounded and secure. This grounding develops in the holding environment of family life and in religious experience. As Thurman said, "[being] cared for and protected and loved in the immediate family provides the firm ground of security for the self" (Thurman, 1965, pp. 5-6). Held in the firm grasp of love, the human being is able to refine, reshape, and redact a more whole and cohesive narrative, and be more fully a person of God. It is really important to note that when holding is less than good enough, the family of faith can repair the developing spirit and ground it in love. Leaders on the border must have the capacity to create a holding environment in which repair and grounding can happen.

Recall that the root of religious experience is the border-space between the mother and the infant. When an individual is held in a good enough manner, seeds are planted for religious experience and reconciling work; they are inextricable. Religious experience sets into motion a process that makes us whole; it is as if we can then see into ourselves, "beyond all [our] fragmentation, conflicts, and divisiveness," and recognize our more real self (Thurman, 1979, p. 179).

Thurman's life with his grandmother, and her faith, taught him the power of love. His living text exemplifies the idea that the way one is held informs one's ability to hold. Good enough holding grounds a person, such that one can take risks and engage in border crossing experiences toward the other. Good enough holding—love—also facilitates trust, "belief in," and hope. Finally, held firmly in love, we can narrate a true self in relationship to others that is accepting and affirming of difference.

Summary

I have been suggesting that the leaders in our study have particular living texts that enable them to hold together the cultural diversity in their congregations. In chapter 1, I briefly introduced the concept of "both/and" thinking to talk about the ability to live with ambiguity. In chapter 2, we discussed DuBois's concept of double-consciousness, or twoness, and the concept of *mestizaje* from Elizondo to talk about an aspect of identity in the leaders: they have multiple narrative voices. I am now asserting that I believe the leaders have also been held in such a way that they are grounded in love enough to take risks, to narrate a whole self, and to accept and affirm the difference in others. Those capacities help them hold together culturally diverse communities by telling compelling stories, gleaning stories from congregants, and weaving together all the stories with God's story. Leaders on the border are *griots*. I used Winnicott's concept of holding and transitional experience, along with an exegetical look at Thurman's living text, to draw those conclusions.

Now, let's look again at Adrienne and Jong Woo, as we think about the ways they were held, the development of their theo-ethics, and how they hold their congregations.

HOLDING AND THE THEO-ETHICS OF CONFLICT AND BORDER CROSSING

Adrienne Brewington

Adrienne's father grew up in the Roman Catholic Church and served as an altar boy. His father was prone to angry outbursts, so his time at the church, full of duty and responsibility, was comforting. These are characteristics he carried with him into adult life. He worked every day, fixing things, taking the children somewhere. Adrienne's dad walked away from a career in music to have a family.

Adrienne's father typified "firm love." He was "distant, protective, and concerned." Adrienne's image of God comes out of her experience with her father. She said, "Dad was such that if you wanted to do something, and could explain why, you could do it. He was near enough to protect you; he might seem like he was not paying attention, but he was."

Being held by a father who was both physically close-by and watching, yet distant and concerned, has formed in Adrienne the ability to hold things in tension. Dad's love was full and complicated, present and distant, firm and permissive, protective and concerned. God, as Adrienne has said, is like that for her. Both parents communicated a sense that "you can do it" and "we will help" that built trust in her environment. Even without much childhood experience in church, Adrienne's trust in her holding environment transmuted into trust in God.

Adrienne remembers falling asleep in a holding environment that included the blue tones of Thelonious Monk, the soft sound of laughter, and the tinkling of ice. Adrienne's childhood holding environment was also occasionally filled with the sounds of bitter arguments between her parents.

They were often conflicted. To her childhood eyes, they did not have a great marriage. But they seemed to value the conflict. Whatever their disagreements were they fought openly. This created in Adrienne an ongoing struggle: the sound of raised voices still "gets [her] back up." She has to remind herself that she is not twelve and to stay in the present. Adrienne's childhood living text was held in an environment formed by a father whose love was firm, distant, protective, and permissive and a mother whose love inspired confidence and supplied her needs. She was also held in an environment that sometimes included meanness, contention, and raised voices. She does not like loud conflict and anger; she looks for ways to talk things through, to reconcile, without rancor, and often with humor. We can say that her passion for reconciliation results from the ways she was held. Adrienne's adult holding environment includes the discovery of God, whose promises are for her, and who, as she says, "works miracles."

The way Adrienne was held affects the way she holds her congregation, particularly the way she holds the reconciliation of conflict. So, for example, living with conflicted parents who both loved her profoundly informs the way Adrienne perceives her role in the congregation. Being literally between two loving, but conflicted, parents made Adrienne a bridge. This metaphor is one carried forward in her ministry. As she put it: "One thing that is part of my job is to not be a reconciler but to be the conduit so the reconciling can take place. I can be the bridge so that it can take place."

Even though Adrienne's parents "could be really unpleasant" and "mean to each other," it seemed to Adrienne that for them this behavior was an acceptable norm. Adrienne's mom also uses denial as a defense when she and Adrienne are in conflict. This capacity for denial in her family storied in Adrienne a keen ethic of "keeping it real." Adrienne's parental holding environment has had a profound effect on the way she holds conflict in her congregation. She survived the conflict, and her parents also "survived" her disapproval. Adrienne knows keeping it real can help her survive. She also knows when to "keep [her] head low, when to keep [her] mouth shut, and when to speak." "You know how not to be baited all the time [into conflicts]," she said. She knows when it is appropriate to stand back and let congregants work it out.

We have seen that although part of Adrienne's holding environment was characterized by tension between conflicted parents, she was also held in the distant, close-by, firm, permissive love of her father and the "I have what you need," "You can do anything" loving container that was her mother. This good enough holding gave Adrienne a profound sense of belief in her parents and herself, and the potential to believe in God. Trust in God is a key aspect of Adrienne's theo-ethics. As she says, "My core theology is 'Trust God.' I know that miracles happen; they have happened to me." Adrienne's congregation notes her deep reservoir of faith as a palpable gift that keeps them together; her faith holds them.

One way to characterize Adrienne's home/container is that it held conflict with denial; she repairs that story in the way she holds her congregation. Another way to characterize her holding is that it was trustworthy enough to engender in Adrienne an ability to trust. Both of these storylines inform her living text, and her leadership in the congregation. Now we turn to the living text of Jong Woo Park.

Jong Woo Park

Earlier in this chapter, we explored how J.W. was held in an environment that included a variety of experiences with flexible borders. Recall that his grandfather bent gender stereotypes, and how that holding environment informed both his father's sternness and compassion. I would surmise that raising children as virtually a single parent gave J.W.'s mother some traditional gender-role diffusion as well. Not only did J.W. experience permeable borders, he is also a border crosser. Later in this chapter we will consider how the way J.W. was held stories his theo-ethics of borders in his congregation.

J.W. has crossed many borders. Raised by an atheist father and a mother who was "a little into Buddhism/Confucianism," J.W. grew up as an atheist as well. He became a Christian in college and started attending church when he met his future wife, Hi Rho. When he came to the United States with his new wife to get a business degree, J.W. attended a small church in which he came to feel called to ministry in the midst of that community. J.W. and Hi Rho have been married for seventeen years, and attended seminary together. They have one child, Felicia, who is thirteen. Her birth is the peak event in J.W.'s life. But his joy was tinged with the reality of prejudice in American culture.

Coming to America meant not only crossing an ocean but also moving from a monocultural context to one in which he experienced racism. Like Thurman, J.W., grounded in the holding love of his mother, has chosen a love ethic rather than anger and violence. When he was appointed to a previous church that was African American and white in makeup, the people felt disappointed that he was Korean. They were wounding and critical. Even in his pain, J.W. had a hope that there was good to come out of the negative circumstance. There was conflict every day, but J.W. became "wiser and more confident. It was God's way to train me."

J.W. crossed economic borders as well. His dad was a general, which meant economic power. A driver took J.W. to school when he lived in the city. "I was treated like a prince, always treated like a VIP," he said. "I thought the whole world was mine. I did not want for anything." J.W.'s dad divided his wealth among his five children. Married and with plans to work in banking, J.W. got his portion, along with a sports car and college tuition. "When I changed to ministry, dad said I broke my contract, so I was on my own." Without his father's support, J.W. worked in roofing in Oklahoma. He and his pregnant wife made a diet of eggs and bread. Grave financial hardship changed J.W.'s life perspective completely. "How precious to labor for your bread," he said.

J.W. is surprisingly not bitter about this change in his life; rather, it resources him and his faith. "I was not angry because dad was fair." After J.W.'s daughter, Felicia, was born, his parents supported the family again. Today, J.W.'s parents, while wishing he worked in a profession less difficult than ministry, "are very proud of me and Hi Rho."

Like Adrienne, J.W.'s childhood holding environment engendered a strong sense of trust. When he was eight, there was a family picnic at a huge lake. As dusk fell, the family spent some time on the shore collecting rocks. When the picnic was over, everyone packed up in two cars and left without J.W.! A child with a sense of humor, J.W. first thought they were joking. He started walking. It got darker and darker. He waited thirty minutes or so. Suddenly there were headlights coming back; it was his family. "Each of two cars thought I was in the other car. I had been thinking, 'Eventually they will find me,' and they did."

J.W. also spent a great deal of time traveling with his family. This literal border crossing stays with him in terms of a theo-ethic of journeying and risk taking. He sees himself as a sojourner who easily crosses borders and who is comfortable managing change. J.W. attributes these capacities to his trust in God. Thus, J.W.'s theo-ethics of borders as safe to cross, like his other storylines, have their root in his childhood holding environment. Like Thurman, whose life was peppered with racism yet buffered by Grandma Nancy's safe arms, J.W.'s life, peppered with the subtext of violence that military life brings, was buffered with the holding of his parents' love. Moving around from place to place to visit his dad is a key metaphor. "I see myself as a sojourner. I like to move around," he said. He said this about change: "And change is another theme. Not only physically, but I change as a person and a pastor. I have confidence and trust in God. This journey is not my own." So, regarding borders, J.W. delights in being a sojourner and thrives on the adventure of change. J.W.'s theo-ethical storyline is informed by the both/and experiences of his childhood, which include crossing borders literally and figuratively. His fluency with border crossing makes him able to hold his congregation, while they cross the borders of sameness to cultural diversity and while they cross the borders of superficiality to deeper intimacy in community.

A core component of J.W.'s theology is grace, typified in Jesus' forgiveness of the adulterous woman. He said, "Jesus knew her sins and was willing to forgive. That really touches me. I know I am not perfect, but I am not hard on myself." Nor, according to his congregation, is J.W. hard on others. His theo-ethics of love, like Thurman's, includes a gracious acceptance of the other based on what I would call *empathic imagination*: the ability to feel the story of the other as one's own. J.W. also has humor to laugh at himself, which translates into the life of the congregation as ease and good-naturedness. His leadership invites a selfless joy and unabashed delight in the other. J.W. speaks of being compelled toward a ministry of reconciliation in ways that are similar to Thurman's urgent sense of the same ministry. A man with permeable boundaries, a man comfortable crossing borders, J.W. says about reconciliation, "I feel called to do this, it is time to do this, and I have the skills to do this."

CONCLUSION

In this chapter, we have discussed the developmental theory of D. W. Winnicott, focusing on the ways good enough holding forms personality. We then examined the ethics of Howard Thurman, whose living text compelled him to want to transform a racist culture into a global community of human beings called to an ethic of love. We found Winnicott and Thurman to be helpful conversation partners, with complementary ideas on holding, love, and human relations. We also were able to use Thurman as a model of leadership, and exegete his living text with our theoretical lens.

Exegeting the living texts of Adrienne Brewington and J.W. Park, we drew some conclusions about how the ways they were held formed theo-ethics of conflict and border crossing. We began a discussion about the holding they do in their congregations, holding that creates a container for the co-authoring of a new group story. In this next chapter, we will exegete the living text of Gordon Dragt, our model leader, applying what we have learned. I will then focus on how Gordon storied a theo-ethic of *radical welcome* at Middle Collegiate Church and help us see how important that capacity is for leadership in multiracial, multicultural congregations. I will also discuss how important it is to be *multivocal*—to speak in tongues—while leading on cultural and racial borders. It is important that leaders communicate welcome, speak the truth in love, create and sustain ministries of social justice, manage conflict, and cross borders toward the other in multiple discourses, so that everyone can hear the good news and have it story their lives.

CHAPTER 4

STORIES ON THE BORDER

TOLD IN MULTIPLE VOICES

INTRODUCTION

In chapter 1, I spoke about how my journey to this book began: at worship at Middle Collegiate Church. That is not quite true; my vision for a reconciled humanity, a Church that is multiracial, multicultural, and antiracist, and a nation in which the scars of racism have diminished is almost as old as I am. It began in my own living text, at five years old, in kindergarten, when I found out that some children thought I was different, and that my difference made them judge me. It was sharpened when I was nine years old, on a field trip with my classmates, as we watched our teacher's face crumple and tears fall from his eyes when the park ranger gave him a certain piece of news. Mr. Smith told us that Dr. King had been killed, and we all wept as well. As I lay under my bed in Chicago, staying away from the bullets that were flying that night, I was convicted that I would work for racial justice in America, so that no one would be judged by the color of their skin. I also have committed my life to the radical welcome of all of God's people to the banquet table in the Realm of God. My own story illustrates how ethics and capacities are *storied* in leaders.

We turn our attention now to Gordon Dragt, my immediate predecessor at Middle Collegiate Church and a leadership model for ministry on the border. When I met Gordon, one of my friends was on staff at Middle. Felicia introduced us, and I immediately felt drawn to this wide-smiling, very gracious, bright, and warm minister. When he agreed to let me interview him for my project, I also found in him a kindred spirit. At first glance, a forty-something black woman and a sixty-something white man may seem to have little in common. That is not true in our case. Among other ways we *twin*, we both were deeply impacted by the life, theo-ethics, and murder of Dr. Martin Luther King, Jr. We both live on many borders, including the border of Christianity and "celebrating the many paths to God." And we both have had the distinct honor and privilege to serve Middle Collegiate Church.

Some would argue that people of color in America, particularly those who have made it through academic institutions and corporations, as I have, must learn to be multicultural and be fluent in several cultural languages in order to thrive and survive. I think that is true. But how did Gordon, who is from the middle of mid-America and who is white and male, learn how to say, "Welcome," to so many different kinds of people in so many different ways? I had a burning curiosity about that when I went to study him and Middle Church.

Before we look at what we can learn from Gordon's journey, let me remind you of some of the ground we have covered. First, recall that I think of identity development as finding one's narrative voice in conversation with multiple, overlapping, and (sometimes) conflicting stories. Second, all of our stories are formed in the context of metastories, two of which conflict: the storyline of racism in America and the gospel story of the realm of God. We have been exploring the ways that visionary, prophetic, and purposeful leaders have some identity characteristics or *storylines* in common. In their living texts, they have a two-ness, or plurality. They were held in such ways that they can hold together differences. They seem to have been held in love, such that they are able to receive the otherness of the other. They are truth tellers; they work for social justice, embrace conflict, and have permeable and flexible boundaries. They cross borders often. In our first chapter, I defined effective leaders as those who tell compelling stories that wrestle with the current stories in the minds of congregants; they reframe the stories, transform the stories, and give them a new ending. Those stories make meaning of where the congregation has been and where it is going; those capacities are critical for change management. In this chapter, we will hear some of Gordon's story. Because we have been introduced to our exegetical sources, I will offer some connections all along the way to the theory and give practical examples of the ways Gordon models what we are learning. Then, I will talk about how important it is that leaders tell stories in such ways that culturally diverse congregants can hear them in their own language. Here is Gordon's story.

GORDON DRAGT: HOLDING, RISK TAKING, AND GRACE

Gordon Dragt was born to Henry and Anna in Grant, Michigan, in June of 1940. Gordon had seven brothers; three are now deceased. The first three were a year and a half apart; six years passed, and then the last four were a year and a half apart. Gordon sometimes considers himself the middle child, and sometimes the oldest of the last set of boys. He has the leadership and entrepreneurial spirit of an oldest child and the peacemaking, conciliatory spirit of a middle child.

Gordon graduated from Hope College in Holland, Michigan, in 1958, and from Western Seminary in 1962. He earned a Th.M. from Princeton Theological Seminary in 1965. Gordon is married to Gayle, whom he has known since they were children. They have two children, Cassie and Duke, and two grandchildren, Mabel and Zebulon. Gordon is a very bright and articulate person who is both/and on many poles. He is confident and humble; he is gentle and tough.

Gordon is gifted and self-deprecating. "I have been described as having many skills for ministry," he says, "but truthfully, I don't have any. I just know how to find people who do." Gordon is serious ("moreso after the car accident Gayle and I had") and very, very playful. After seminary, he went to see *Zorba the Greek* with a colleague who thought of Zorba as a "Christ figure." Gordon learned what it was like to "get the *Zorbic* quality inside, to get chaos and celebration inside." That Zorbic quality shows up also in Gordon's alter ego, Rainbow the Clown, as whom he has performed professionally for many years. "I am always looking for ways to communicate, for new ways to open doors. The real clown comes from inside, no matter how I am dressed." One sees the *Zorbic* quality in Gordon as he moves through the congregation, greeting members with a warm hug, or as he sits in the fellowship hall, giving everyone a taste of his infectious smile. One congregant says, "I don't know what it is about Gordon, but when you stand near him, you feel his joy and you know you are loved."

When Gordon was about five years old, he had a vision that still both moves and embarrasses him. "I keep it to myself; it does not fit into my theological frame." It was summer and he was at his parents' cottage on the lake. He was coming back from Sunday school with his brothers, riding on a dirt road. He had a vision in which he saw a being, which his child-self would have called *Jesus*. This encounter with what he would now call "a spiritual being" made Gordon feel both anointed and protected. "I did a lot of foolish things," he said, "but I feel God called me. So, no matter how I tried to mess up, God would not let it happen."

The confidence Gordon has in God's ability to keep him from falling grounds him and gives him the ability to innovate. He knows how much that capacity shapes his leadership style and helps grow Middle Church. "*The New York Times* described Middle as the place 'where old-time religion gets new twists.' That is me." Some people focus on Middle's new twists, but Gordon is really clear that congregants need to have both identifiable, familiar, grounding and new, fresh, and surprising ways to image the good news. In other words, as leaders narrate the new story, connecting it to the old is part of what makes it compelling; it is part of what authorizes the new story. "I always keep one foot firmly planted in the center, but the other is dangling over the edge." As an example, Gordon arranged for a choreographer to use several ten-foot-tall puppets to tell the Palm Sunday story. "People who come for worship will find the familiar. The order of service and the story will be familiar, but they will also be surprised by the spectacular, amazing new twists."

This centered risk taking comes from the way Gordon was held at home. He is absolutely fearless because of his mother's gracious acceptance and his father's willingness to take risks. Anna was very loving, very patient, and gracious. "I could never be out of her favor. No matter what I did, she always let me back in, and embraced me." Gordon's theoethics are shaped by that gracious mother—God is grace, God is acceptance, God is welcoming—Gordon both believes that grace and behaves that grace. He also brings into his ministry this sense of patient grace by *paying the rent*.

Patiently and graciously being with people and building relationships pays the rent so that visionary innovation is well received. "One must be a good pastor and a visionary in order to have lasting influence [power] and little conflict," Gordon said. Congregants say that for the longest time, when the church had fewer members, Gordon went to brunch with everyone after worship. As the church grew, Gordon moved from table to table in the Middle Link Fellowship Hour, spending time with people after the worship celebration. He playfully calls the time with people, "the ministry of schmoozing." About the worship, Gordon says, "I don't call it a worship service; every Sunday is a celebration and should be joyous." That joyous celebration spilled out into the social hall, and Gordon connected with people in small groups to check in about the week, rehearse the celebration, and convey a radical welcome to all.

Gordon's mom, Anna, was also the disciplinarian. Just as it was in Karen's household, Gordon says, "If one of us got in trouble, we all got in trouble. Maybe I did not start it, but

I was responsible to stop it." That sense of what is right and wrong stories Gordon's ethic of social justice. He feels an ethic of responsibility to right the social ills in our culture. He is also very disciplined and consistent in his work ethic. Gordon's father, Henry, was courageous and encouraging and had a great entrepreneurial spirit. "Dad was always proud of me, and of course I learned a lot from him." Everyone who walked into any of Henry's stores was treated like a "king or queen." Even the migrant workers were able to have credit with Henry; none of the other merchants did that. Henry storied in Gordon a radical acceptance of the other; all of God's people are to be treated with dignity. He also storied in him a boldness that sometimes takes Gordon to the edge of the church. At a time when The Christian Reformed Church demanded that its members not watch television, Gordon says, "Everybody had them, but they would hide them when the preachers came over. My dad built our house on the hill, and put the television antennae right up there. He told the truth about who we were."

Henry started several businesses while Gordon was growing up; he was never afraid to try something new. This is a trait of Gordon's ministry; he always tries to start "three new programs a year. If they don't work, try something else. It is important for the community to see me trying to reach out to them." One of the businesses, Henry Dragt's Trade O'Rama, became a regional attraction to which people as famous as the Gerber family and people as poor as dirt would come. Henry had a clientele that was economically diverse. Gordon's congregation is like that. Gordon's radical welcome of all peoples is storied by both his mother's grace and his father's success at accepting racial, ethnic, and economic diversity in his business establishments.

We have discussed how our storied selves are formed in the larger stories in culture. Two important *plot points* in history served to story in Gordon some key theo-ethical commitments: First, the Vietnam War storied in him a commitment to peace. One of the first outreach ministries at Middle Church was PeaceTalks, committed dialogs and action toward peace in America and around the world. Second, the assassination of Martin Luther King, Jr., storied in him a commitment to multicultural ministry. "Never again would I serve a unicultural congregation." Gordon has been purposeful in extending a welcome to the city of New York in all its diversity. When Gordon first came to Middle, there were only twenty-one or so people worshiping there, mostly Ukranian and Polish. Gordon was discouraged at his first worship celebration. He went across the street to a bakery and had a vision that "all the stones on the front of the church became doors through which diverse persons would walk." Gordon became a welcoming doorman. He had learned in Bucks County, Pennsylvania, that other multicultural churches grow; that proved to be true of Middle. In Pennsylvania, Gordon crossed the border to the Arthur Hall African American Dance Company and built a partnership with them. "People did not like it; we did it anyway."

Then, in 1971, Gordon found himself facing another border. There were really great people in his congregation who were gay. "I had gone all along in my education, never thinking about this. All of a sudden, I did, and I thought, 'so what?'" The commitment to full inclusion of all persons is central to Gordon's ministry. He says, "People need to have important experiences with people who are different than they are. Making that happen is an important part of my ministry." Through the arts in worship on Sundays at Middle Church, people have had extraordinarily important experiences together. Puppets, dancers (not liturgical dancers, but tap, ballet, modern, and jazz dancers), jazz musicians, gospel singers, classical singers, and great preachers all story the Realm of God in extraordinary and transformative ways. A new group story is being authored at Middle Church, as culturally diverse people hear the good news in a cultural language familiar to them.

Leadership in multiracial and multicultural congregations means helping people have important experiences together. As people worship together, work together, and play together, congregants become friends and appreciate each others' differences. "We learn to appreciate what each of us brings to the community," Gordon says. Leadership in multiracial and multicultural congregations must help congregants rehearse the reign of God, to create a common history and future, and to create together a new congregational story. In order to invite and encourage their congregants to do that, leaders need to be able to articulate that invitation in multiple discourses. They need the capacity to be *multivocal*; *they must speak in tongues.*

SPEAKING OF SPEAKING IN TONGUES

Black feminist literary critic Mae Henderson's work offers helpful language with which to reframe and reiterate my thesis that the plurality, or *mestizaje,* of the self gives leaders the capacity to engage in multiple discourses or multivocal storytelling. Henderson writes about the *simultaneity of discourse,* by which she means the ways the perspectives of race and gender and their interrelationships simultaneously structure the discourse of black women writers. In her essay "Speaking in Tongues: Dialogics, Dialectics, and the Black Woman Writer's Literary Tradition," Henderson describes the *dialogic* character of black women's writing, saying that it reflects not only a relationship with those who are culturally other—men, women of other cultures—but also "an internal dialogue with the plural aspects of self that constitute the matrix of black female subjectivity" (Henderson, 1990, p. 118). Black female writers, she argues, are always addressing the other, the internalized others, and the multiplicity of selves. Because each social group speaks its own unique language in which they express shared values, perspectives, and norms, writers must communicate in many languages, which she calls heteroglossic voices. Henderson also argues that not only are black feminist writers speaking in many voices, the goal of their communication is twofold: one is to build consensus with the other, and the second is to contest and tear down walls. So there is a duality of purpose in the communication, a dialectic in the dialogue.

What Henderson concludes about the plurality and simultaneity of discourse that is characteristic of black women writers is true of our study leaders. For example, Adrienne's gender-same discourse with white women in her congregation is simultaneous with her race-different discourse with the same cohort. She discourses in a dialectic of sameness with African American men, and in a dialogic of difference with them as well. At the same time, she participates in a contestorial dialogue with ways racism and classism affect the holding environment in which her church grows, as she tells a compelling story/vision that confronts race, gender, and class oppression in the community. It is a story, so confirm her congregants, which offers a vision for genuine human community and for healing that human community of its divisive insistence on separation.

Our study leaders hold together multiple storylines in their identities by developing narrative voices that speak in simultaneous discourse both with others and with their own internalized other(s). For example, Karen is multivocal in that she is conversant in the languages of many cultures; she converses in English; Presbyterianism; educated-in-graduate-school speak; Spanish; African American cultural idioms; American cultural idioms; blue collar, white American idioms; and Spanglish, to name a few. With those dialects, she is helping story a new group identity for her congregation in their language. The leaders can do this because they have the capacity to not only read (in) and discourse with the language of the larger culture, they also can read (in) and discourse with the cultures that belong to their various congregants. This significant leadership capacity enables the clergy leaders to tell the compelling story/vision in ways that cohere to, or fit with, each congregant's own story. Part of what makes the story "fit" is that the leaders tell the story in a "plurality of voices as well as a multiplicity of discourses," so that each congregant can hear the emerging story in her or his own (cultural) language. Thus, the clergy leaders in our study have *mestizaje,* multivocal narrative voices (identities) that enable them to embrace the complexity of difference in diverse communities and to story a moral imperative to value diversity to their congregations. This capacity is what Henderson calls *speaking in tongues*, a term she borrowed from the church.[1] We are borrowing it back.

One interpretation of the Pentecost event is that it is the undoing of the event at the Tower of Babel (as recorded in the Hebrew Scriptures, in Genesis 11), in which humans, unable to understand one another, fell into discord, and were scattered. The miracle of Pentecost is that the gathered could hear the same good news—in their own language; that miracle built the church community.

Multivocality: The Pentecost Paradigm

Recall that leaders tell and enact compelling stories that wrestle with the stories that already reside in the hearts of followers. Congregants are not blank slates on which to be written; they listen to leaders' stories through the filter of their own living texts, and the most effective stories are the ones that fit. By fit, I mean, does the story make sense? Can it be appropriated, in this time and in this place? Is it authentic, coherent, and believable? Does the leader's life embody the story he or she tells? In order for leaders' stories to have coherence and authenticity, "It is important that they know their [own] stories, to get them straight, to communicate them effectively, particularly to those who are partial to rival stories, and above all, to embody in their lives the stories that they tell" (Gardner, 1995, p. xi).

How does one tell a story that "fits" in a diverse context? It must be multivocal. It must (1) speak with integrity to the living text of each person at the table of fellowship, (2) be able to be understood in their "language," and (3) help build an emerging group story. It must help build a common *mestizo* language that enables congregants to tell stories to one another and move away from superficial relating to authentic community.[2] It must story a new border ethic. Because these clergy leaders successfully hold together multiple narrative voices (Schafer, 1992), they tell fitting stories that form identity in the midst of diversity.[3] The stories reflect the culture and the historic time and place; they critique current norms and values, and point the way to new ones. This is a critical capacity for leading on the new religious frontier.

It is appropriate, then, to reappropriate *speaking in tongues* as a metaphor for the *mestizaje,* multivocal, multiple-discoursed storytelling to which I have been referring. Our study leaders tell stories that not only reform the current identity stories of congregants; their stories also critique and reform hegemonic cultural stories. As they do so, they use a plurality of voices (including nonvocal storytelling, which is enacting as opposed to narrating) that hold the congregation in such a way that each congregant can hear the emerging new story in his or her own language. Further, once congregants are reformed by the story, they too become narrators of the new vision. There is a sense of conversion on the border (culture changes us; we change the culture) that liberates and engages congregants to be change agents toward God's vision of shalom. Congregants, then, help co-author the new story in emerging border languages.

Thus, multivocal storytelling in emerging *mestizo,* border languages is an essential leadership competency required on the new religious border. Border leaders help author a new group story in their congregations, as they weave together congregants' stories with stories from sacred texts that call forth a new story/vision. The emerging new story disrupts, revises, and transforms the story of separateness and homogeneity. It reaches back to the culture of the early church and revives the story of a multicultural community. It is eschatological in that it rehearses a future in which all people praise God in one voice. Further, the new story helps critique and transform the American cultural story, which has been historically woven with segregation, inequality, racism, classism, and sexism: the new story is countercultural. Storytelling on the new religious border, then, means leadership that is disruptive, deconstructive, revisionary, and reconstructive.

How did our study leaders come to have this capacity? We have seen that our leaders have had different developmental experiences. What do they have in common? Karen is literally *mestizo* but is also culturally *mestizo.* She straddled

racial and ethnic borders as a young person, and continues
to do so in her ministry and in her biracial marriage. Randolph's experience with Retha as an "other-mother" was
foundational to his racial identity development. Even
though he had few cross-cultural experiences outside of his
home, he straddled borders inside his home as he was held
by Retha. Both he and Karen have an internalized other
voice, which gives them a strong sense of empathy. Jong
Woo straddled cultural and economic borders along his development. Adrienne grew up with black parents and siblings but often went to white schools; she too straddled
borders and does so today in her ministry. She talks openly
about her inner white girl, an internalized other voice. Gordon's family straddled religious borders; they were more liberal and risk taking than their other Christian Reformed
counterparts. Gordon says that he continues to "keep one
foot firmly in the center, while the other dangles over the
edge."

Writing about black women writers and oppressed peoples, Henderson says that they develop the ability to speak
in multiple discourses in response to the racism in American culture. The writers are double-conscious, she indicates.
What Henderson argues about black women authors is
analogous to what I am arguing about our study leaders.
Held in American culture, they have all, like Elizondo and
Thurman, regardless of race and gender, developed a
double-consciousness, or plural identity, and the capacity to
tell multivocal stories.

Our clergy leaders have the capacity to dialogue internally
with and externally from their multiple selves. They have a
mestizo consciousness (Anzaldua, 1987), or a self-conscious
border identity; they hold two or more identity storylines together, the result of which is the emergence of a third new
storyline. And, per their own testimony, the leaders in our
study both deepen their sense of identity as *mestizo* and
bring their identity to greater consciousness every time they
revisit or rehearse their story. These clergy leaders, like feminist Gloria Anzaldua, Virgilio Elizondo, and others who
straddle borders and who consciously hold together multi-

ple storylines, and value them, might be called *border people*. As Anzaldua says, "Living on borders and in margins, *keeping intact one's shifting and multiple identity and integrity* [italics added], is like trying to swim in a new element, an 'alien' element.... The 'alien' element has become familiar—never comfortable, but home" (Anzaldua, 1987, p. iii).

One can wonder if there is a cultural prescription for us here, a way for leaders to develop this border consciousness and with it a multivocal capacity. What kinds of conclusions can we draw about the identity development and attributes of leaders, not only clergy leaders but also leaders in all sectors, who are able to do this border crossing work? I think one conclusion we can draw is straddling borders can form in leaders the capacity for multivocality. Further, all leaders have the opportunity to straddle borders. We can choose to put ourselves in self-conscious, empathic contact with the other. Even those leaders who live in what seem to be monocultural contexts can be self-conscious about creating border experiences from which to learn.

Leaders on the border are multivocal, a capacity that enables congregants to hear, in their own cultural language, the compelling story these leaders are telling, and to develop a new group story in an emerging *mestizo* language. It is a gift that enables them to address both commonality and universalism, and difference and diversity. Following are brief examples of how the study leaders' multivocality enables the culturally diverse members of their congregations to hear the compelling, theo-ethical story/vision they tell in such a way that it fits.[4]

LEADERSHIP, THEO-ETHICS, AND THE STORIES LEADERS TELL

Multigenerational, black, white, and brown, Karen's congregants agree that Karen tells an authentic multivocal story in worship, literally infusing her sermons and worship music with Spanish. She also stories a passion for God and the ethics of truth telling. One of Karen's members said, "I can get blown away by the warmth, the singing in different languages. Karen is so authentic." Karen leads an exciting blend of worship and leads the church into the community. "I like our services. They are [both] old/traditional and new/praise. There is new music, and Christian rap. Karen models that we are an action-oriented church."

For Karen, one of the compelling stories that hold people together is that they are connected in a need for healing. She teaches her congregation that brokenness is a "truth to be told." As I shared earlier, Karen has "no hair on [her] tongue." Almost all members, regardless of age, gender, and racial and ethnic identity, affirmed that Karen "teaches that God calls us to reveal our brokenness and be in touch with it so that we can use it to minister to souls ... if we are honest, we are so much more alike!" "Karen always calls it. She says, 'let's put it on the table and talk it through.'" "You can tell Karen anything; she really wants to hear it." Karen's message is consistent, "in her sermons and in meetings," and in her life. Even with Karen's candor, some members fear telling the truth when they disagree with policy, lest they appear to be unsupportive. In the main, however, most members of Westminster hear from Karen a consistent, compelling theo-ethical story about truth telling that "fits"; they try to live out that story.

Comments on Randolph's leadership were often about the story he enacts. Gay and straight, male and female, wealthy and poor, black and white—members from each of the three worship services agreed that Randolph models what he preaches. They said, "Randolph never looks down on anybody." "He not only preaches about justice, he does it. Look at our ministries. How many churches have a homeless ministry? And now we are going to start the school for adults (English as a second language)." "When you look at the group of people [leading] in the front, they are very different [from one another]." Randolph stories[5] the theo-ethics of social justice not only in the sermons he preaches, but also in his behavior.

Recent elections to the vestry are evidence that the congregation is participating in the new group story of cultural diversity. A gay man and two black women were elected, prompting members in the study to say, "Randolph doesn't just say that he believes in diversity, he models it in his leadership, and expects it of us. Electing two black women and a gay man? If that is not [culturally] diverse, I don't know what is." Thus, Randolph tells a nonverbal story/vision to his congregation that values diversity and social justice.

Adrienne tells and enacts multivocal stories in worship. With her presence, she tells a nonverbal story of joy and serenity and a deep well of spirituality. She creates a container for self-reflection on inner conflict and for interpersonal conflict as well. As her congregants say, "Adrienne has a deep spirituality, a deep reservoir of faith." "Adrienne is the best thing that ever happened to us." "Adrienne is deeply spiritual and is clearly called by God. Her spirituality pulls us together." Adrienne calls the church to confession in an intimate whisper, "How was your week? How is your soul?" All the members in focus groups affirmed that Adrienne tells a story of God's forgiveness and grace that creates a safe container for conflict.

Another story that Adrienne tells is embodied in her own candor and directness, which makes space for congregants to enact the same behavior. For example, Adrienne resolved a conflict in her congregation over monetary issues by allowing everyone at the meeting table a time to speak, "no matter how long it took," she said. "Everybody has to have their say, and I can be patient with that." Adrienne's congregants get to have their say, so that conflict does not brew underneath the surface of relationships, and Adrienne has her say as well. One female congregant, angry with Adrienne seemingly for just being a woman, and black, stopped speaking to Adrienne and stopped acknowledging her. "She did not look at me, she did not address me; she looked past me," Adrienne said. Adrienne gently confronted her, "You will talk with me; it may take time, but I am not going anywhere." Members of Westbury United Methodist Church affirm that "Adrienne is so direct, she tells you exactly what she is thinking. She tells you with humor, though. She has a great sense of humor and is able to laugh at herself as well." Thus, the multivocal stories Adrienne tells, stories of forgiveness and of making space to hear one another, create a holding environment in which members can coauthor a new group story.

Both J.W. and his congregation believe that because he is Korean, he is uniquely able to tell stories that hold them together. As one congregant observed, "The mere fact that J.W. is Korean works for us here. I think it was a deliberate choice [by the bishop]." Although J.W. is perceived as neutral because he is neither black nor white, his Korean cultural experience brings unique particularities to the context. Being both conservative and a relatively new and seeking Christian (former atheist with Buddhist/Confucian leanings) helps him tell compelling, fitting stories to those whom J.W. refers to as "the more conservative blacks" in his congregation and "the more liberal whites." A certain cultural "humility" and "gentleness" makes room for members of Fairhaven to "take ownership" of the ministry. Because of the flexible boundaries with which J.W. grew up, J.W. holds his congregation with optimistic stories of harmony, peace, and flexibility. He says he is able to do this because he "does not draw lines, there is a zigzag; the boundaries are not clear" and he is "open to new ideas." J.W. is what might be called a "boundary extender."[6]

J.W.'s congregation affirms that the story he tells is one of harmony and peace. They describe his core theo-ethical story as one characterized by "togetherness, by word and example." "J.W. has a real spiritual life and cares about each of us individually." The congregation finds comfort in J.W.'s biblically based call to "living right" and to "inclusion." He is perceived as "very sincere." J.W.'s theo-ethics both broaden and deepen the spirituality of the community. Further, both J.W.'s complicated (*mestizo*) theo-ethical storyline, and his Korean racial, ethnic, and cultural heritage stretch the boundaries and definitions of race and religion in America. Things are no longer black or white (Smith, 1981, p. 147). Congregants say, "When J.W. first got here, what we all agreed was that he was difficult to understand, with that accent. Now, he is just one of us. He has such a great sense of humor." "I agree, and actually, his accent makes you listen; you really have to pay attention to what he is saying. And when you do, you hear his humor and his spirit." Thus J.W. stories the theo-ethics of boundaries to his congregation in ways that fit with each congregant's cultural story.

Gordon told stories to Middle Church both in the language of tradition, or old-time religion, and in the language of innovation, or vision, "new twists." He speaks the language of welcome in many dialects. He is consistent, warm, open, affirming, and intentional in welcoming all of the people who come to Middle, just as they are. He opens doors through a ministry of humor and surprise. He preaches the gospel through the arts in worship and through social action and outreach. He says, "God loves you," every time he pays the rent.

Gordon manages the inevitable conflict that comes with diversity with the same language of welcome. "We may not be on the same page, but I get people working together. If a crisis does come, then my policy is to take care of it immediately. Address it right on—don't let it simmer." People trust Gordon even when they disagree with him.

We have seen that in each of the study congregations, what the clergy is intending to *story* is being heard across the different cultures represented. For example, the aging white man; the Dominican younger mother; and the middle-aged, married white women all hear Karen "telling" stories about truth telling. The new African American couple, both partners in recovery, celebrate along with the oldest member of the church, a seventy-year-old white man, that Adrienne is the greatest gift to the congregation because she is authentic, warm, and deeply spiritual. The older, black matriarch; the older, white matriarch; and the younger, black gay man all admit how difficult it was to understand J.W. at first, but now they love him and think his deeply biblical sermons and his sense of humor make him a good leader. And even though some people critiqued him for too much honesty, the white, middle-aged gay man; the middle-aged, African woman; and the executive, single white woman believe that Randolph "walks his walk and talks his talk" consistently with all the members in each sector of his congregation. In the rich diversity that is Middle Church, one of the unifying aspects is the respect congregants have for the uniqueness of the other, respect storied by Gordon in his preaching, his worship leadership, and in his very person. So the leaders' capacity to be mulitvocal helps build unity in diversity.

We also see in each of the leaders a healthy ability to be authentic and to embrace conflict. Adrienne is "direct," and Karen "has no hair on [her] tongue" and speaks the truth. Gordon sits down and works it out right away, so that even if someone disagrees with him, they will trust him. Randolph is criticized for being too honest, and J.W.'s sense of his father's fairness is storied in his ministry in that he mediates conflict by giving everyone a little of what they need. These leaders are not conflict adverse, and they listen, listen, listen!

In this next chapter, we will talk more specifically about the multiracial and multicultural ministry at Middle Collegiate Church, both during Gordon's ministry and in mine. We will talk about preaching and worship, teaching, and leadership development. We will talk about visioning, planning, and intentionality about changing culture. We will talk about leading on the border and the Pentecost Paradigm.

CHAPTER 5

ENACTING THE
PENTECOST PARADIGM

LEADING AND HOLDING: A BRIEF REVIEW
OF LEADERSHIP STUDIES

Before we explore our model of leadership at Middle Church, it is helpful to have a brief, broad review of the field of leadership studies. The first leadership theories in the nineteenth century, the *trait approach,* focused on great men and their impact on society. In response to that position, theorists argued that history has more to do with leadership than the traits of the leader. In other words, theorists like Herbert Spencer (1884) argued for a *situationalist approach* to leadership. The times produce the person, they asserted, rather than the person producing the times. In the latter part of the twentieth century, theorists synthesized the trait and situationalist views, arguing that different situations demand different leadership approaches. The next innovation was that theorists began to study the *transaction* between leaders and followers; they focused on how leaders gained and sustained influence. For example, Howard Gardner's approach to leadership is a transactional approach, where the transaction is the compelling story that is told and received as a source of identity.

Adaptive Leadership in a Multicultural World

By most census projections, white people in America will be in the minority by the last half of the twenty-first century. Leaders in all sectors of public life face the challenge and opportunity to work with ever increasing diversity in their workplaces.[1] This means that in many cases, leaders will have to engage in *adaptive work*, which requires innovation to "address conflicts in the values people hold, or to diminish the gap between the values people stand for and the values they face."[2] Adaptive work involves learning new behaviors and requires a secure holding environment to manage the conflict that comes with change.[3]

Leading on cultural borders is adaptive work. Creating a sense of security while constituents navigate change and conflict is a capacity leadership needs. Certainly as leaders work on culturally diverse borders and seek to replace segregated silos with authentic, culturally diverse communities, conflicts arise. The new vision critiques the old. The old wineskin cannot often hold the new wine. When the status quo is changed, tension is produced. Leaders need to know that although tension and disequilibrium are motivators for change in organizational structures, they also need to be managed with care.

Leaders who are intentional about embracing cultural diversity also must be intentional about creating a holding environment in which change can be well managed. Practically speaking, just like a caregiver knows how to hold a developing child, an effective leader in adaptive situations needs also to hold constituents and their developmental challenges as they grow toward the new vision. Leaders on the border must also help contain the emotional issues in groups as they navigate cultural borders, embrace new ways of being, and manage change. So creating a holding environment for the management of conflict, change issues, and emotions in a multiracial and multicultural community is a capacity that leadership on the new religious border requires.

Our study leaders taught us about some of the ways they hold their congregations on the border. Karen's theo-ethic of truth telling creates an environment of trust. Randolph's uses social justice issues as a way to hold his culturally and economically diverse community together with a common focus. Adrienne's management of conflict stories an attitude about conflict in her context that keeps people together. J.W.'s self-effacing humor and management of borders through compromise holds his congregation. Gordon's radical welcome and relationality held Middle on the border. Those are some of the ways our study leaders create a container for work on the border.

When I began this study, I was a senior consultant at the Alban Institute. Along with my consulting practice, I led a team studying how leaders negotiate cultural boundaries. One of the ways our team learned about leadership on the border was in a conversation group with clergy leaders working in multiracial and multicultural congregations. We read books and articles together, and had structured conversation about the capacities leaders need on the border. Along with the capacities I have already discussed, here is what our group decided leaders also need.

Leaders on the border need

* The ability to bring critical analysis, a faith tradition, and learned articulation to bear on the situations we see.
* The willingness to be wrong.
* The courage to speak the truth and to know when to be quiet and listen.
* The courage to deal with conflict, including the dissonance between our expectations of both God and humanity, and reality.
* The ability to communicate when there is conflict and the ability to create community in the midst of it.
* To know where the border is. Borders shift contextually and leaders have to discern where they are.
* To be self-reflective, be open, and take in information.
* To be aware of the self and the other, which is to be *emotionally intelligent*.

* To have the bold, visionary, prophetic spiritual willingness to act when action is not popular, knowing that de-
liverance is coming.
* The ability to live on the border in the midst of tension
and death.
* Humility.
* Allies.

Summary

I am saying that leaders who have the capacity to tell *multivocal* stories in multiracial and multicultural contexts will increase the possibility that the compelling story will "fit" with
the living texts of followers. Because the story fits, it is more
likely that the emerging story will be understood by the followers, and that they will make the story their own. I am referring to this multivocal way of leading on the border as the
Pentecost Paradigm. Leading on the border is adaptive work,
so leaders must create a container in which conflicts can be
negotiated, emotions can be experienced and addressed, and
the new compelling story can be heard. In other words, border leaders must hold congregants' anxieties and tensions
in the borderspace between the "now story" and the "not-
yet story," as it emerges.

In the case of building multiracial and multicultural congregations, the "not-yet story" is one of increased cultural
diversity. In another adaptive situation, the new story might
be of increased productivity or environmental stewardship;
it may be a story of increased international partnership or
being a better urban neighbor. No matter what the new story
is, it is important that leaders in all sectors be aware that they
tell the new story through their own story; leaders must be self-
aware of their "stuff." The awareness of self and other, *emotional intelligence,* is an especially critical capacity for
congregational leaders because they have so much power to
impact the living texts of others.

The adaptive work of building a multiracial and multicultural church is often the result of some disruption of the
status quo. The neighborhood has changed. Membership has

declined. The hearts of the congregational leaders have been convicted that a monocultural congregation is no longer a viable option. A new church development has been commissioned that will be intentionally multiracial or multicultural. The disruption produces both anxiety and excitement. In order to move toward a new vision, the current reality must be accurately described, then deconstructed and revised before the required reconstructive work can take place. Let's now look at how that process took place at Middle Church.

PREPARING FOR A PROCESS OF CHANGE

There are many places of excellence in Gordon's ministry that we could review. For example, we could look closely at the twenty years of ministry he had before he came to Middle Collegiate Church. It is helpful for this conversation to focus on times when Gordon encountered events at Middle that disrupted the status quo. First, Gordon went to Middle in 1985 at a time when Middle was in decline after a long pastorate and an interim; his call to Middle was a disruption! There were twenty-seven people in his first worship celebration; Gordon felt disappointed and a little depressed. From across the street at Moishe's bakery, Gordon looked back across at the front of Middle and noticed all the stones on the face of the building. He had a vision that the stones turned into doors "through which people could come. My job was to keep opening doors." That vision informed Gordon's strategy for ministry. How many doors could he open for people to enter? How many entry points to the ministry could he create? And when people came in the doors, would they see themselves represented?

Redeveloping and transforming a congregation takes time. "You have to plant the seeds, water the seeds, and watch them grow," Gordon said. "It takes eight to ten years." By 1993, Gordon and the consistory of Middle were working from the following mission statement:

MISSION STATEMENT OF THE MIDDLE COLLEGIATE CHURCH
11-8-1993

The Middle Collegiate Church is an historic Protestant church dedicated to celebrating and living the gospel of Christ in the East Village on the Lower East Side of the city of New York, with national, global, and universal concerns in mind.

In the story of the Great Banquet, Jesus spoke of inclusion and hospitality. The good Samaritan parable reminds us that disregarding people with different heritage or experiences from our own is wrong. Welcoming all people is the gospel. Therefore, Middle Collegiate Church is committed to being an ecumenical inclusive congregation that celebrates the rich pluralism of the human, social, and urban environment.

This commitment is expressed in the mission of the Middle Collegiate Church by being a friendly, vibrant center of the community and city with a diverse ministry of worship, music, spiritual growth opportunities, acceptance, compassion, community involvement, and a celebration of the arts.

Key components of Gordon's door opening vision were

1. Worship as celebration. The niche that Middle created in the city of New York was, "the East Village church with worship as celebration." Essential to celebration was a commitment to the arts in worship and in the life of the church. Dance, puppetry, jazz, and gospel music were new languages in which the gospel could be heard. A young actor named Jerriese Johnson came to Middle and asked to start a gospel choir. Gordon gave permission, and the gospel choir helped transform the life of the congregation. In the celebration, Gordon preached a word of hope. His core sermon was that God loves you just as you are and that you are welcome here and in the realm of God. He told that story in mul-

tiple voices: in the music he chose, in the texts he selected, and in the ways the culturally diverse staff and board (*consistory*) represented inclusion. Committed also to inclusive language, Gordon was notorious for changing the lyrics to songs to make sure they were appropriate!

2. Partnerships with the community. Gordon spent time connecting with the community. He attended community board meetings, "schmoozed" with local vendors and civic officers, and helped start three outreach ministries per year. One such ministry was actually started by a member. The Celebrate Life Meal began in 1987 and is an ongoing ministry at Middle Church, serving seventy meals each Monday to persons living with HIV/AIDS. Some other outreach programs included PeaceTalks, an annual street fair to benefit the Celebrate Life Meal, and an annual float in the Gay Pride March each June.

3. Partnerships in the church and with colleagues. The Collegiate Church is the oldest continuous protestant denomination in America, dating back to 1628. The five current ministries are really one church on five campuses and have a built-in collegiality (hence the name *collegiate*); Gordon worked closely with colleagues at what were then four congregations and with the local judicatory, the Classis. His commitment to serving on committees and boards and to being a good colleague meant changes at Middle excited and inspired the system, rather than threatening it. The changes and growth at Middle Church would not have been possible, for example, without support from its closest collegiate neighbor, Marble Church.

4. Paying the rent. Gordon created a holding environment for change by building real relationships with the existing congregation. In his first year of ministry, Gordon joined the Women's Fellowship as the only male member. Even as Gordon began to travel to teach and share Middle's story, he committed to being at Middle every Sunday, unless he was on vacation. He held the congregation by always being there and by touching lives on Sunday morning in the Middlelink Fellowship time in the social hall (playfully called the ministry of *schmoozing*). By paying attention to the

current membership, he created a holding environment for the change. Feeling cared for, having their voices and feelings heard, the older members of Middle embraced the new vision and the newcomers it brought.

5. Prophetic commitment to radical inclusion and diversity. Gordon and the consistory were committed to being a multicultural and multiracial community in which all persons were welcomed. The community of the East Village was multiracial and multicultural and also diverse in sexual orientation. So the doors were open to all, and people came. Middle was not the "gay church" like some in the city, but the church in which singles, families of all configurations, straight, gay, and all people worshiped together. It was the place people went when others rejected them. It was the place for recovering Catholics and Baptists. It was the place for those who had given up on religion to come and be healed and to have joy.

In summary, then, Gordon's arrival at Middle disrupted the status quo. He created a vision for a preferred reality, and the consistory supported it. The core story was "you are welcome." Gordon deconstructed the old paradigm and revisioned a congregation in which worship was celebration, and the arts were a source of multivocal storytelling. Gordon created a container for change by paying the rent, caring for the current congregation, and connecting to colleagues and the community. Gordon was intentional about staffing the vision with a racially and culturally diverse team, which included paid staff and consistory members. Gordon was innovative and permission giving when it came to outreach to the community.

If there were any growth edges in the twenty years of ministry Gordon did at Middle, they are these: (1) There might have been more opportunities for spiritual development and education for adults. Gordon says, "That is not my gift; but I know we need to do that." (2) There might have been a more consistent ministry to children and youth. The East Village has changed several times in the last twenty years. A thriving after-school art program served families during the week, but it has been difficult (and it still is) to sustain a consistent children and youth ministry. (3) Gordon might have changed his leadership style as the church grew from program sized to corporate sized. Developing leaders and developing staff are places where Gordon says he could have pushed harder.

Under the leadership of Gordon Dragt, Middle Church grew from twenty-seven people in worship to 350; from thirty-five members to 550 members in twenty years. Its budget grew, its endowment grew, and its commitment to the community grew. Middle's influence in the church has been tremendous, as students have come from as far as the Graduate Theological Union to study worship and the arts. Gordon's ministry has been featured in several publications, including the much acclaimed *Beyond Worship Wars,* by Tom Long. Gordon's ability to be emotionally intelligent—self-conscious, purposeful, intentional, and self-reflective; to know the needs of others in an adaptive situation—is an incredible capacity for leadership.

Even Gordon's ability to know when to retire (he calls it "the timing of my time") was an incredible insight from which we can learn. Sometime in 2001 or so, Gordon began to envision where Middle's next horizons were. He began to believe that the next new heights would require new capacities in leadership. "I hate plateaus," he says, "and I can smell one when it is coming." Anticipating his retirement and his replacement became the next disruptive moment in Gordon's ministry at Middle Church.

Disrupting the Status Quo

Gordon was sixty-one years old when he began to imagine that he might retire from the church he transformed. He absolutely could work longer and "do a great job," he said, "but there were places I wanted Middle to go for which new leadership was required." Although Gordon did not widely publish that decision, he and the consistory began to plan for ministry at Middle without Gordon.

In order to plan for change, Gordon and the consistory conducted an *internal audit*. They asked questions of identity and values. Who are we? What do we stand for? How do we do the things we do, and why? After some careful and thoughtful conversation, the consistory established a document called "The Essential Spirit of Middle," which described their identity; *they narrated the current chapter of their story*. Here is what they described:

THE ESSENTIAL SPIRIT OF MIDDLE
Middle Church Consistory
Revised 10-24-2002

Informality of Style
Changing / Evolving
Friendliness / Expression of Openness / Welcome
Acceptance / Affirmation of Diversity of People
Importance of Seeing People Who Are "Like You" in
the Pews
Maintaining a Balance in the Midst of Diversity
Giving a Voice
Diversity of Staff / Consistory / Congregational
Leadership
Sustaining Effective Communication
High Quality of Worship / Worship as Celebration
Diversity of Worship Expressions / The Use of the
Arts in Worship
Diversity of Belief
Balance Between the Biblical Foundation and
Everyday Life
Balance Between the Reflective / Intellectual and the
Emotional / Feeling Expressions of Faith
Balance Between the Traditional and Pushing the
Boundaries of What a Church Can Be
"One Foot Planted Deep in the Center and the Other
Dangling Over the Edge"
Reformed Church in America, yet Ecumenical in
Spirit and in Practice

Missionary to the Denomination / Broader Church
Involved in the Neighborhood / Reaching Out
to the City
Concerned about the World / Justice / Spiritual
Engagement with Social Issues

Notice the polarities, or both/and nature of their self-perception. Middle's leaders saw themselves as balancing the biblical witness and the experience of everyday life. They saw themselves as RCA and ecumenical, as traditional and pushing at the boundaries. Not surprisingly, much of their identity-story reflects who Gordon is. Leaders do shape congregations through (and in) their own image, so it is important to be self-conscious. Gordon's grounded risk-taking helped story Middle's identity. As the leadership at Middle took a new look at their identity, they imagined who would be the kind of person to lead them into the future.

ESSENTIAL MINISTRY LEADERSHIP
Middle Church Consistory
Revised 10-24-2002

People person / likeable
Genuine / welcoming
Personable / friendly
What does the person's diversity include?
Communication / relationship skills
Can deliver an effective sermon for the Middle Church congregation and within the total environment of Middle's worship celebration
Can the person supervise / manage within the designated ministry responsibility?
Can the person do the "business" of the church / give attention to details?
Is the person an administrator?
Can the person balance and effectively function within both the "essential Middle" and the "essential Collegiate"?

Can you imagine the person as a minister at Middle Church?
Are the person's leadership skills large enough?
Are the person's relationship skills broad enough?
Does the person have skill for working in a ministry team environment?
Does the person have a "command person" quality?
What are the person's attitude and habits toward doing the work of ministry?
Does the person have a vision for Middle Church and for ministry?
Can the person translate vision into reality?
What is the person's commitment to the "essential Middle"?

Next, after the consistory talked about their identity and the kind of leadership they might need, they imagined the next place on their journey. They began to do some visioning.

SUCCESSION / MIDDLE VISION / 2002

Rethink entire use / allocation of current church house space
Creatively expand current facilities
Develop Middle as a "teaching church"—seminarians, arts ministries, transforming the local church
Becoming a city-wide church based in the East Village, not just a neighborhood church
Additional worship celebrations
Stronger adult education programming
Consider a larger variety of small group ministries—develop more ways for people to enter and participate in the life and ministry of Middle Church
Develop an off-site entertainment ministry
Create a teen ministry that reaches out to the neighborhood and city
Create more young adult spiritual programs
Develop a Middle Church Interfaith Ministry

Start a Middle Church Bookstore
Consider a broader media ministry—broadcast, printed, radio, movie, video, CDs, and so on

Middle's consistory and the consistory of the four ministries embarked on a search process the year before I came to interview Gordon. I was the fortunate person who got called to serve at Middle as Associate Collegiate Minister. It was our hope that I would succeed Gordon, if all went well. We overlapped in our ministry for eighteen months, with a strategy that I would gradually take over more of the ministry at each six-month interval. Sharing ministry with Gordon was a joy! He was a generous, creative, and extremely capable colleague. We respected and loved each other and had so much fun planning for the future.

One of the things that I learned from my consulting practice at Alban and from reading congregational leadership sources is that a clear and compelling vision can create a holding environment for managing change. I was especially helped by *Church Leadership*, by Lovett Weems. A clear, compelling vision is critical when leaders are changing culture and moving a congregation into the future. The vision helps communicate a direction and to create a container for managing change. So, equipped with initial vision conversation by the Middle consistory and my research in the congregation, I set out to do one-on-ones throughout the system to hear the passions of individual members and to do a visioning process with the congregation. Our process also included focus groups with congregants, staff, and the consistory and conversation with community members. Below is a broad description of our process; see appendix A for more details in visioning.

WRITING THE VISION, MAKING IT PLAIN: A DISCUSSION ABOUT THE PROCESS

This is the group process I have used with governing bodies and staffs of congregations in my consulting practice and at Middle Church.

First, I create a container for the work through education and structured conversation in the staff and on the board. We establish a common vocabulary and normalize expectations about conflict and change management.

Second, I use a narrative frame in order to help the group do *visioning*. For example, a few of the questions we answer are

1. If our current reality is a chapter in a book, what is the title of the chapter?

2. As you envision an ideal ending for this story, what is the title of the next chapter?

3. As you analyze the gap between the current chapter and the desired next chapter, what are the major plot points that need to occur in order for the ideal outcome to happen? What resources are needed to make them happen?

4. What is the work you need to do on in order to create a container or holding environment in which the work can happen?

Visioning is best done in a retreat setting but could take place over several meetings. At Middle Church, the consistory and staff started the process in separate meetings, and then joined together for a retreat to build the team, share information, and complete the process.

Third, the governing body commissions a *vision team* consisting of staff, consistory members, and people from the congregation. The team should be representative of the cultural diversity in the congregation and be commissioned to do three things:

1. *Collect internal data* from written sources (like worship attendance, enrollment in classes, and so on) and in focus

groups in the congregation. I usually train the team to run focus groups in teams of two and ask questions like these: (a) Which program, event, or ministry at this congregation is most helpful to you and your family? (b) If you could add one thing to the ministry we do here, what would it be? (c) At this church we say we are committed to _____, but I think we could do that even better. These questions serve as an essential descriptor of the current ministry. I also train the team on facilitating a focus group and give them a listening guide for collecting the data. I ask each pair to translate data from flip chart paper to a computer document and then interpret the data by asking themselves: (a) What surprises us? (b) What new insight do we glean from this group? (c) What is one implication for our process?

2. *Collect external data.* Along with the written data mentioned above, I have used several methods to gather external data: I have invited community members in to talk in focus groups; I have interviewed key partners, like the principals of local schools, community board chairs, leaders from other faith groups, and so on; or nonprofit organizations, like music schools, who are stakeholders in the community. The questions I ask them are about community perception: (a) What is the story you hear about our congregation in the community? (b) If you were working closely with us, what is the one thing you would want us to do differently? (c) When you imagine a church being a partner in the community, what is the one thing it would do? Besides conversations with stakeholders, external data is gathered from sources like PERCEPT Data, which resources congregations about their demographics; local school data about enrollment K–12, by racial and ethnic breakdown over a five-year period; and data from local real estate patterns.

3. *Produce a draft vision statement.* The *vision team* culls together the data and produces a *draft vision statement* with the instructions that *a vision statement should be descriptive of who we are five (or ten) years from now.* It is helpful for the statement to be able to answer the question: In five years, in the community of our church, we see _____.

4. *The governing body and staff then discuss, revise, and approve the statement.* The *vision team* then produces goals, objectives, and action plans which are prescriptive of how to achieve the vision. They present those to the governing body for approval. The governing body should then present the vision statement and goals to the congregation and staff in an interactive meeting, for buy-in. The agreed-upon vision helps create the container in which adaptive work takes place. When in doubt, I like to say, "The vision is the boss of us; it is our covenantal path to the future."

A visioning process should take at least six months to complete. Visioning is not a static process because congregations and the communities they serve are dynamic. At Middle, we began our process during Lent in 2004, while Gordon was still with us. We approved our Vision 2010 plan in March 2005. We continue our process with annual retreats and quarterly congregational conversations to share information and to update our data. We evaluate with the congregation: this is what we said we would do; how are we doing? Who are we today, who is our community today, and how does that inform our call? Staff work on goals and objectives, and create a six-month plan for their work. A permanent lay-led *vision team* bears the vision and holds us all accountable to our plan, *Vision 2010*.

We have said that congregational leaders' storytelling in their congregations is impacted by their own stories. My own story of life on the border on Air Force bases makes me passionate about multiracial and multicultural congregations. My storyline as a psychologist of religion also makes me convicted about deeper community in culturally diverse communities. Whereas some might imagine the development of a multiracial and multicultural congregation as a continuum, I image it as a spiral of ever deepening relationships with the self and with the other. In my vision, congregants move from surface relating in worship to deep communion with one another. The vision of a deeper, more authentically relational community stories Middle's vision statement. Imagine a *V* on its side. I envisioned our community not only growing out and wide into the world, but growing down deep both in community development and personal spiritual development. You can hear that in our goals, if you listen for it. Here is how I see it.

THE PENTECOST PARADIGM:
A Spiral of Deepening Relationships

Worshiping in a Monocultural Congregation
Awareness of the Desire to Diversify
Strategizing to Create a Culturally Diverse
Worshiping Community
Worshiping in a Culturally Diverse Congregation
Choosing to Come to the Fellowship Table Together
Choosing to Share Stories at the Table
Choosing to Listen to Stories at the Table
Allowing Stories at the Table to Inform or Change
One's Living Text
Worshiping in a Multivocal Congregation
Allowing Stories at the Table to Coauthor a New
Group Story
Stories at the Table Change the Nature of the Table
Table Talk and the New Story Go into the Homes of
Congregants
Worshiping in an Antiracist Congregation
Table Talk and the
New Story Go into the World
New People Are Invited to the Table
New People Do the Inviting / Power Shift
Choosing to Come to the Fellowship Table Together[4]

When I envision Middle's future, I see us moving from a multivocal congregation to an antiracist congregation. We are working together to coauthor a new group story. We are engaging in small group conversations and educational opportunities that change the nature of our community, "our table." We are hearing that members are telling their family members about life at Middle and risking taking on racist attitudes.

I have used this schematic with groups to help them evaluate where they are on the spiral, to name where they want to go and to think of the strategies they need in order to get there. It might be helpful to you, as you seek to become more deeply engaged in the multiracial and multicultural work on the border.

Here is the vision statement we developed, and our first draft plan. Note how the goals and objectives roll right out of the vision statement. Staffing, budgeting, and resource deployment should roll out of the plan as well.

MIDDLE CHURCH VISION STATEMENT
Adopted March 6, 2005
By the Middle Collegiate Church Consistory

Middle Collegiate Church is a celebrating, culturally diverse, inclusive, and growing community of faith where all persons are welcomed just as they are as they come through the door. Rooted in Christian tradition as the oldest continuous Protestant church in North America, Middle Church is called by God to boldly do a new thing on the earth.

As a teaching congregation that celebrates the arts, our ministries include rich and meaningful worship, care, and education that nurture the mind, body, and spirit; social action that embraces the global community; and participation in interfaith dialogue for the purpose of justice and reconciliation.

Growth/Diversity

Goal 1: Reach new and different neighbors in the city through *worship* and *outreach*

(In the main, outreach has as its aim bringing people to Middle to experience God's love; mission or social action has as its aim taking God's love out into the world.)

Objectives:
1. Add a second celebration on Sunday afternoons targeting the after-brunch crowd
   a. May be two demographics: under thirty and baby boomers
2. Evaluate, revise, and increase participation in Soul-Care Wednesday worship—focus on seeker cohort
3. Use media ministry to stream worship celebrations
4. Establish relationships with campus ministries at local universities
5. Establish high school arts outreach
6. Reestablish arts ministry team for outreach (and inreach)
7. Greater use of 7th and 2nd Gallery as outreach

Deepen Spirituality / Mind Body Spirit

Goal 2: Establish Middle Church as a center for *care (nurture)* and *education* (a.k.a. *teaching congregation*)

Objectives:
1. Develop MiddleCares ministry
   a. Membership retention and development
   b. Pastoral counseling
   c. Prayer and sharing opportunities
   d. Create help / counseling / life coaching center
   e. Staff the ministry
2. Increase and diversify the number of small groups
   a. Train teachers
   b. Enlist outside teachers
3. Increase and diversify adult education offerings
   a. Evaluate and revise
4. Increase number of ministry teams and participants

5. Increase local participation in arts and worship course
6. Develop spirituality and leadership course as offering for non-Middle and Middle lay leaders
7. Develop course on multiracial and multicultural congregations for clergy, lay leaders, and seminarians
8. Utilize web site for
   a. Prayer requests
   b. Inspirational messages
   c. Life coaching

Social Action / National and
Global Presence / Interfaith Dialogue

Goal 3: Establish social action ministries at Middle Church with global, national, and local emphases

Objectives:
1. Evaluate, revise, and build upon current local outreach (Celebrate Life, seniors, and clothing and food drives)
2. Research and develop program to involve Middle community in local, national, and global social action projects
3. Evaluate, revise, and build upon PeaceTalks for global, interfaith program on social justice
4. Establish social action ministry team to research and develop global project

Goal 4: Establish media ministries at Middle Collegiate Church

Objectives:
1. Explore Marble and other models
2. Meet with vendors to receive media proposal
3. Create budget for media team
   a. Purchase equipment for media room
4. Hire staff
5. Redevelop and enhance web site

a. Stream worship
6. Redevelop print materials
7. Evaluate and enhance advertisement

Resourcing the Ministries

Goal 5: Acquire additional space in the East Village for Middle Collegiate Church

Objectives:
1. Partner with the Collegiate Corporation to purchase neighboring property
2. Reconfigure new and existing space for staff offices, youth and college meeting space, and fellowship space
3. Reconfigure new and existing space for classrooms, large meetings, breakout classrooms, and media center

Goal 6: Reconfigure and acquire staff for Vision 2010

Objectives:
1. Hire children and youth staff person
2. Add staff to maintain Middle's commitment to both education and nurture and diversity
3. Shift current staff for new objectives
4. Hire part-time JJEV Gospel Choir director

Goal 7: Embark on stewardship and partnership campaign for Vision 2010

Objectives:
1. Present plan to congregation for buy-in
2. Prepare budget for 2005/2006 and draft for 2006/2007
3. Invite congregation to partner with vision in series of educational and homiletical events
4. Create Middle-appropriate materials for stewardship campaign
5. Launch special giving opportunities, beginning with Gordon Dragt Arts Fund

PREACHING THE VISION IN WORSHIP

For every Sunday in worship, the staff and I plan an artistic worship celebration that stories the vision for Middle Church. If Gordon's ministry was characterized by "welcome," my ministry is characterized by "welcome, and...." If Middle's previous mission was directed at flinging open the doors to the community, our current vision has our doors swinging both ways. Not only are people welcome just as they are as they come through the door, we send people out—transformed and healed, ready for mission and outreach. My core theology is "God can and will, with our partnership." I preach a gospel of radical love, of radical welcome, and of radical justice. I try to find the unusual in the familiar stories in the Scriptures.

Using the lectionary schedule, I ask every Sunday, "what is God requiring of us this week, for ourselves, for others, and for the world?" My simple exegetical process is to ask the text, "When? Where? What? Specifically what? So what? Now what?" As I move from exegesis to sermon, I have in mind also the exegetical work I have done in the living texts of my community. Edwin is in marital trouble; Keith is starting a new job; Janine has lost her grandmother. The Care Team is in training; the course on race is winding down. And of course, I exegete the culture. Images from pop culture, current events, and hopes and dreams for our world populate my sermons. I read current literature, fiction and nonfiction; I see movies and plays; I listen to a wide range of music, so I can stay in conversation with the texts with which my people are in conversation.

In the "so what" and "now what" parts of my sermon, I address in very practical ways what the people of God can do in terms of making a way where there is no way. The God I image is not looking for puppets; God wants partners. I stretch people, I know. I am Christian and universalist. The Jesus I preach is a socialist border person who is more interested in pulling people into God's plan than leaving them out.

I ask my staff to use the lectionary to preach their ministry areas. I preach the larger vision, but my care minister will preach care; my mission and social action minister will preach mission, my education minister may preach the importance of parents as the first preacher at home.

An Arts Ministry Team works with me to tell the story creatively. A puppet show, a drama, or a dance may work alongside the sermon to preach the good news. Two choir directors collaborate with me to make sure the story we tell is a cohesive one. Take a look at our bulletin from the first Sunday of Advent, 2006. Building on Gordon's frame of an Advent Dance that expanded each Sunday, the Arts Ministry Team and I decided to create Advent Events that would highlight different artistic expressions.

In the first celebration, we used dance. We also storied our diversity by using two versions of a piece from Handel's Messiah, the traditional version and one more contemporary to which a very exciting dance was choreographed. We held together old and new in a very creative way.

Sunday Worship Celebration

December 3, 2006 • 9:00 | 11:15 A.M.

Familiar Hymns, Songs, and Spirituals

— GATHERING —

PRELUDE	*Of the Father's Love Begotten*	Eric Thiman, composer
HYMN*	*Now Is the Time Approaching*	New Century Hymnal

PRAYER OF THANKSGIVING*

— Worshipers may be seated —

ADVENT EVENT	*But Who May Abide? (Messiah)*	G. F. Handel, composer

INTERGENERATIONAL DANCE

— Children dismissed for Children's Church —

ANTHEM	*But Who May Abide? (Messiah)*	G. F. Handel, composer

WELCOME

MORNING PRAYER

LORD'S PRAYER (Middle Church adaptation)

> Ever-loving God, hallowed be your name. Your reign
> come, your will be done, on earth as it is in heaven.
> Give us this day our daily bread, and forgive us our
> sins, as we forgive those who sin against us, and lead us
> not into temptation, but deliver us from evil, for yours
> is the reign, and the power, and the glory, forever.
> Amen.

— REFLECTING —

SCRIPTURE	Luke 21:25-36	
SERMON	*The Power and the Glory!*	Jacqui Lewis

— RESPONDING —

OFFERING	*E'en So Lord Jesus Quickly Come*	Paul Manz, composer
COMMUNION	*Call to Advent*	Jerome Williams, composer

DOXOLOGY/DEDICATION*

> From all that dwell below the skies
> Let faith and hope with love arise.
> Let peace, goodwill on earth be sung
> Through every land, by every tongue.

HYMN*	*Mine Eyes Have Seen the Glory*	New Century Hymnal

BENEDICTION*

PASSING OF THE PEACE*

POSTLUDE

— *Indicates please stand if you are able —

On the second Sunday of Advent, we focused on music. It was my idea to have an "opera," in which most of the liturgy was sung, and in which the music was as diverse as we are. Our Middle Church Choir sang classical pieces, our Gospel Choir performed gospel music and spirituals. We had a jazz vocalist sing a prayer, and a rhythm-and-blues musician sang a popular song as a prayer of lament. That same musician accompanied my spoken-word sermon.

Sunday Worship Celebration

December 10, 2006 • 9:00 | 11:15 A.M.

Musical Meditation
— GATHERING —

PRELUDE	*A Rose Breaks Into Bloom*	Johannes Brahms, composer
INTROIT	*Lo, How a Rose E'er Blooming*	arr. David Leavitt
HYMN*	*We Hail You God's Anointed*	New Century Hymnal
PRAYER OF THANKSGIVING*	*A Child Is Born*	Jones/ Wilder, composers

Jazz Solo / Piano Accompaniment

ADVENT EVENT	Candle lighting by Seniors

— Worshipers may be seated —

WELCOME	Jacqui Lewis

MORNING PRAYER / LORD'S PRAYER
(Middle Church adaptation)

Ever-loving God, hallowed be your name. Your reign come, your will be done, on earth as it is in heaven. Give us this day our daily bread, and forgive us our sins, as we forgive those who sin against us, and lead us not into temptation, but deliver us from evil, for yours is the reign, and the power, and the glory, forever. Amen.

PASSING OF THE PEACE*

— REFLECTING —

SCRIPTURE	Luke 3:1-6, 15-18	
Jerriese Johnson East Village Gospel Choir	*I'm Gonna Sing 'Til the Spirit Moves in My Heart*	Moses Hogan, composer
	I Thank You Lord	Mattie Moss Clark, composer

103

SERMON   *What Shall We Do?*   Jacqui Lewis
                                                      and Myke
                                                      Henni

—RESPONDING—

OFFERING/   *Every Valley Shall Be Exalted*   John Ness
OFFERTORY   Beck,
                                                      composer

DOXOLOGY HYMN / DEDICATION PRAYER*
    From all that dwell below the skies
    Let faith and hope with love arise.
    Let peace, goodwill on earth be sung
    Through every land, by every tongue.
HYMN*   *Glory, Glory, Hallelujah*   New Century
                                                      Hymnal

BENEDICTION*
POSTLUDE
          — *Indicates please stand if you are able —

A ROAD MAP TO THE SERMON
"WHAT SHALL WE DO?"

The following sermon was in the spoken word genre. It was mulitvocal.

Myke (musician) . . . . . Introduction to "What the World Needs Now"

Myke . . . . Four bars of "Strangers More Than Friends"

Jacqui (preacher) . . . . . *Introduction* (with Myke playing): This text has caught the imagination of songwriters from different genres. I am thinking now of that song from *Godspell*

Jacqui and
Myke (musicians) . . . . "Long Live God"

Jacqui . . . . And we are all familiar with
Handel's *Messiah*

Myke . . . . One bar from "The Hallelujah
Chorus"

Jacqui . . . . Why did this vision capture
the imagination?

Maybe because it is a compelling vision of a preferred
reality. . . .

John the Bapist preaching to a
people who need to see the
world differently, a people de-
spondent, and a people with
little hope.

John wanted the people to
know that the there was one
coming, one who wouldbap-
tize not with water but with
fire that the current world
order was not going to
survive.

So reaching back into Isaiah's
prophecy (in ch. 40), John is
preaching a word of *hope* that
talks about balancing scales,
about evening up the playing-
field.

The picture of mountains
made low and valleys exalted
is a *metaphor for God's sure coming reign.*

Myke . . . . "Make It Funky"

Jacqui . . . . *Transition:* Why did they need hope? Why did they need a new vision?

Why do they need hope? Because they have been invaded by the Roman authorities, and they are living in occupied territory.

Why do they need hope? Because what is ironically called the Roman Peace, the *Pax Romana,* has created what we would today call a military industrial complex.

Why do they need hope? Because the funds usually reserved for education, healthcare, and clean water have been diverted to create roads, build chariots, and make weapons for war.

Why do they need hope? Because the poverty and hardship of the life that they endured in the desert was nothing compared to the abject utter despair they endured after the Romans occupied Judea.

Why do they need hope? Because their religious leaders had been engaged by the Romans to keep them oppressed; the language and attitude of the faithful co-opted to justify the war, the occupation, and the oppression of those on the bottom.

Sound familiar?

John was a prophet, with a calling and a strange outfit, and he was a great preacher, too. The people were so moved by the sermon, so convicted by the sermon, they asked what shall we do? *What shall we do?*

Jacqui . . . . *Transition:* John did not mince words: here is what you do:

Myke . . . . "Bridge"

Jacqui . . . . If you have two coats, give one away.

If you have food, you must do the same.

Even the tax collectors came to be baptized. He told them, "If you have been cheating folk out of their money, if you have been over-taxing them; stop and don't take more than is really required.

When the soldiers came, yes, the Roman soldiers came, he said, "If you have been taking bribes form people by threats or false accusations, give it a rest. You don't need any more than you have already. Be satisfied with your salary."

John's sermon was a sermon about *repentance*, about *turning away* from old things and about turning toward new ways of being. And it was about more than individual change; it was about changing the way we do business. It is a sermon about economic justice.

If we are talking about repentance, if we are talking about *change . . .*

Jacqui . . . . *Transition:* What do *we* do?

Myke . . . . "Make It Funky"

Jacqui . . . . Some of you are thinking, *We don't have any money; I am barely making it.*

Some of you are thinking, *I am already giving a lot; I hope she isn't asking for more.*

Some of you are thinking, *I feel powerless to make a difference.*

The gospel is about evening things up.

Poverty is relative. Some of us have so very much, and some of us are really struggling.

And unfortunately, when people are poor, the ones who suffer the most are children; 121 million children all over the world are not in school, suffering from disease, sent out to work because they are poor.

Fifty-seven million people died last year; 10.5 percent were children; 98 percent were from the developing world.

The text is plain; all of us, right here, right now, can make a difference.

No matter who we are, no matter what our economic status is, here is what we do:

We can donate money to our favorite charity.

We can buy two less coffees per week and use the savings to sponsor a child in the developing world.

We can write to our senator or representative about passing laws that provide a better life for our children.

We can think of love as an active verb.

Myke . . . . *Ending:* "What the World Needs Now," up-tempo.

TEACHING THE VISION

When I first joined the staff at Middle, I taught thirty classes in one year! The idea was to get to know people, and so I offered classes that I thought might be interesting to a broad range of people. *The Artist's Way* used Judith Cameron's book to bring together a group of women for conversation. I taught a class called *The Good, the Bad, and the Ugly: A Study on Mark's Gospel and Evil*. Teaching storied for Middle Church that education is important.

In the second year of my ministry, as I became senior minister, I decided to be more focused in my offerings. I wanted to teach the courses that were longer in duration, that gave more of a chance to build community, and that storied our core theologies and ethics. For example, I taught a class called *Sex and the City,* and focused on an ethic of sexuality that honors God and our bodies. I taught a class called *Spirituality and Leadership,* and used many of the concepts in this book to help leaders both in the church and in their secular environments think about a theology of leadership. I taught a class called *Race, Grace, and the Reign of God* that gave participants a chance to talk about racism in the culture and in the world. That class has been offered three times now, and each conversation gets deeper in intimacy and more edgy in content. This is the tough conversation we want to have as people of God in a safe place.

My staff and I storied for Middle members that learning together is important. We then asked them what they wanted to learn. Recall that it was our goal to be a center for nurture and education. Here is the program we put together for this year. Three years ago, we had two classes. The year I came, I did all the teaching. Now look at what God is doing! We even have brunch seminars at one of our favorite restaurants; we really are putting education on the border too. We have partnerships with several seminaries on our multiracial congregations course in April and teachers coming from around the community. We are storying a leadership role for ourselves and putting ourselves in relationship with people who can share in a mutual, beneficial relationship.

Middle Collegiate Church Adult Education

Following are the scheduled classes for 2006–2007.

Adult Bible Study: 10:00 A.M.

This is a year-long lectionary-based Bible study taught by one of our members. The classes are designed to cover a range of Bible-based texts and their interpretation.

Living the Word: 10:00 A.M.

These are a series of intimate and discussion-based classes that help you understand not only the word of God but its relevance to the world today. They start the first Sunday of the month and run the entire month.

October:	Uncovering What We Believe: Guilt, Grace, Confession, Hope, and Forgiveness
November:	Setting Personal Boundaries
December:	The Parables
January:	The Ethics of Martin Luther King, Jr.
February:	Where the Bible Came From—Oral Tradition to Canon
March:	Where the Bible Came From—How to Read the Bible
April:	Uncovering What We Believe: Sin, Salvation, Faith, Church, and Ministry
May:	Theological Conversations
June:	Parenting for Health and Wellness

Brunch Seminars: 1:00 P.M.

These are a series of special seminars taught in a more in-formal setting. With good food, great teaching, and hearty discussion, be prepared to listen, learn, and talk. All at a great deal—only fifteen dollars for full buffet and drinks.

1. *Gulf Coast Renewal* (all proceeds go to Common Ground—Gulf Coast Recovery)
2. *Cynic's Guide to God: Finding Hope in a Hopeless World*
3. *The Spiritual Life and the Ethical Life—Part I (at Middle Collegiate Church)*
4. *The Spiritual Life and the Ethical Life—Part II*
5. *Making a Plan for Your Life*

Leadership Seminars: 1:00 P.M.

Middle Collegiate Church is one of the leading multi-racial and multicultural churches in the United States. These seminars have been developed to create a shared learning environment and to explore issues of faith, leadership, and diversity in American culture.

1. *Race, Grace, and the Reign of God*
2. Advent Study—*Living the Questions*
3. *Deconstructing "White" in a Multiracial World: Building Just Communities*
4. Lenten Leadership Study—*The Leading Edge: Dealing with Differences and Conflict*
5. Teaching Church Event—*The Power of Stories: Developing Multiracial and Multicultural Ministry*
6. Teaching Church Event–LGBT Conference

Retreats

Discovering Your Personal Power—One-day retreat

DEVELOPING LEADERS ON THE BORDER IN THE CONTEXT OF CARE

I cannot do this ministry by myself, and I would not want to. At our size, over six hundred members and worshiping with about 450 people, I need to spend 25 percent of my time mentoring staff. I do that. I meet with staff members weekly to build relationships and to check in on the progress of our plans. I plan worship with a team. Staff meets biweekly for fellowship, prayer, production of worship preparation, and calendar check-in.

More than just paid staff, I have a great staff of volunteers. Our consistory meets monthly for business but also for on-going training. We most recently had a unit on care during times of transition. I meet with them in one-on-ones to build community and find out how I am doing. I encourage staff to meet with consistory one-on-one twice a year for the same conversation. Staff and I develop other leaders by placing them on ministry teams and supporting them in one-on-one meetings. We have no committees at Middle, just teams, some with longer lives than others. When we spot talent and gifts, we encourage them. I ask potential leaders to take my annual Lenten Leadership Conversation and to register for our longer, more intense courses.

Perhaps the most important way we develop leaders at Middle Church is that we are here together on the border. Multiracial and multicultural congregations are, in my opinion, the hope for ending racism in America. Here in congregational life together, here sharing in the fellowship hall, here worshiping and praying together, we are rehearsing the realm of God. We do it in church school; we do it in adult education. It is more difficult, but we are working on it in our youth programs. We had a painting party one day where our youth from different races and classes decorated their new youth room together. The youth were black, white, and Hispanic. The music was Latino and hip-hop. The painting was as varied as they were, in their parallel play. It is a start.

Our care ministry is growing alongside our educational ministry. On any given Sunday, several people sit at the

Middle Cares table and address cards or make baskets for members. Small groups meet to talk about grief and transition in their personal lives. Our Stephen Ministers have gone to training and will graduate this April and join our two ministers responsible for different aspects of congregational care. All of us spend time in the sanctuary and in the social hall continuing Gordon's ministry of schmoozing, creating a container of care as we move toward an antiracist future. Our Wednesday night SoulCare informal worship keeps loving arms around Middle people so that as we preach more outreach, more justice work, and more racial justice, people feel the space to come along with us. The staff and I take time to talk with the people so they know where we are going and why. In our Calling All Members Project, each congregant is being asked, "how are you, and how are we?" Change is hard for most people, and as we grow, keeping people close at heart is an important skill on the border.

SUMMARY AND CONCLUSIONS

Perhaps one of the greatest gifts this study gives is the opportunity to investigate the living texts of five congregational leaders whose theo-ethical development and religious experience are such that they morally value cultural diversity. At a critical time in history when shifting demographics join with ever present racist, sexist, classist, and heterosexist oppression to make the American cultural landscape a difficult one to negotiate, we have in this project an intimate study of several individuals who have a self-conscious border identity, who see themselves as both called and compelled by a moral imperative to lead in multicultural and multiracial settings, and who story a vision of human relating in which others are compelled to value cultural diversity as well. We have asked, fundamentally: what is it about these leaders' storylines that compels them to morally value cultural diversity and to invite others to do the same? Further, we have asked: what can we learn about their development that will help develop other leaders on the border?

We have learned that living on the border of acceptance and rejection and on the border of belonging and being excluded helped form a narrative voice that stories inclusion for others. We have learned that negotiating geographic, class, and race and ethnicity borders at early points in development creates in these leaders an ability to live with ambiguities. We have learned that our leaders all have plural identities, tell multi-vocal stories, and have developed a *mestizo* consciousness. They have, in other words, multivocal narrative voices. We have learned that the ethics of welcome, conflict, boundaries, truth telling, and social justice are formed in particular holding environments, and that the ways one was held affect the holding environment one creates.

All of these learnings from our study leaders are critical for leading on the border. On the new religious frontier, where greater cultural diversity is the norm, our study leaders offer an intimate view into their development and into the border ethics required for a future of justice and equality for an increasingly diverse and demographically complicated culture.

The identity development of our leaders is a phenomenon that scholars, practitioners, and educators need to study in preparation for this millennium. This project offers a narrative frame for understanding the development of leadership that morally values cultural diversity. Further, it uses that narrative frame as an explanation for how pastoral leadership might coauthor this moral vision with others. In other words, the congregations in the study are laboratories in which we can study how a theo-ethical vision/story of breaking down cultural barriers becomes part of the living texts of congregants as they coauthor a new group identity.

This book provides a narrative lens through which to understand how pastoral leadership affects the religious life or theo-ethical storyline development of congregants. We have learned that our study leaders tell the compelling moral story in a *mestizo* language, one in which each congregant can hear the story in their own cultural language. Speaking from and through their various internalized "others," our study leaders have the capacity to speak to the others in their congregations in ways that are meaningful and sustaining of healthy development. These leaders, as all clergy do, encounter their congregants at critical times in their developmental stories and individual histories. Birth, death, life, rites of passage like baptism or confirmation, weddings, divorce, and other transitions—in all of these life events the clergy leader helps make meaning of the experience. In other words, they do interpretive and coauthoring work, as they use storytelling to build community.

All congregations are holding environments for both shared and individual religious experiences; some of those experiences occur at very vulnerable moments. In multiracial and multicultural churches, vulnerabilities can be heightened by personal histories of exclusion, rejection, or disenfranchisement that can come to the fore when other aspects of our psyche feel exposed. Our study leaders are able to build community and create a safe holding environment in the midst of the opening and healing of ego or spiritual wounds. They minister to psychosocial needs in these contexts. The ways they were held affect the way they hold these congregational needs. This project offers an opportunity to study the whole concept of self-as-leader in these kinds of settings where wounds of the spirit, hurts, and unresolved issues and differing God images or theo-ethics all are on the table for people. In other words, there is something about the complexity of diversity in a congregation that requires from leadership a unique empathic capacity; our leaders have that.

We have seen that our clergy leaders create holding environments in which difficult, adaptive, and potentially conflicted work takes place. They also hold the texts and behaviors, through their passion and regard for them, which encourage the ethics of truth telling, social justice, healthy conflict, and appropriate boundaries. Good enough holding in congregations enables transitional religious experience in potential space. These experiences are transformational. They help the congregation imagine and reimagine their lives as whole, loving, and empowered. As tellers of stories and interpreters of texts, leaders are restorers of hope and carriers of vision. Thus, congregational care creates a holding environment in which transformation can take place, for preacher and for congregant. Leadership in multiracial and multicultural congregations and other contexts requires good enough holding of a particular multivocal quality.

In each of the congregations, there is a sense that the leaders have helped create a safe space for this kind of community. All five congregations, who see themselves and their clergy as "loving and sincere," used the words "home" and "safe haven" and "support system." In some way, perhaps less conscious at times than others, these leaders *switch* language codes. Like Anzaldua, their discourse encompasses many languages that are appropriate for the border that is the new religious frontier. This is a capacity all leaders need in an increasingly culturally diverse world.

Class differences, language differences, cultural differences, and generational differences cause occasional tensions in our congregations. Yet there is a common commitment to something larger than the self that holds the people together. At Adrienne's church, they spoke of it as a love ethic. Adrienne says the work is not hard. "We are supposed to love each other. Love is easy."

At Fairhaven, J.W.'s church, there is a clear commitment to staying together. As one leader said, "What congregations need to do this work is commitment—like a marriage, you stay together and work it out; you keep coming back to the history of relationships." At Epiphany, a similar sentiment was expressed. "What holds this together? We get smarter as we get older. As you get older you find that race and culture are not that important. Community is why we do this." And, at Westminster, friendship is one of the ties that bind. "No one can convince me that we are the same, but we don't let our different journeys and different ethnic experiences divide us. We don't validate racial ethnic identity; we validate each other as friends."

These congregants express what Howard Thurman has articulated so eloquently. Human beings want to be known and loved in relationship to others. In order to be fully loved, we must be in relationship. "The concern for reconciliation finds expression in the simple human desire to understand others and to be understood by others" (Thurman, 1965, p. 164). According to Thurman, it is very simple, very relational. It is about using our imagination to put ourselves in the place of the other.

Why has it been so difficult for humans to do this? Perhaps in a racist culture it is natural for survival to segregate on Sunday morning for support and encouragement (DeYoung, et al., 2003). Race, class, and gender oppression in American culture (West, 1999; Cannon, 1995; hooks, 1990) leave many Americans feeling disenfranchised and in need of great care that might be better sought in safe silos apart from the other. Certainly, pluralism and multiculturalism have their critics (Appiah, 1998), and arguments for monocultural churches make some sense (DeYoung, et al, 2003). Studies on multiracial and multicultural congregations celebrate the success of these churches (Foster, 1997), and provide excellent case studies and resources (Kujawa-Holbrook, 2002; Peart, 2000), but stop short of an analysis of leadership development. I hope this book helps fill that gap.

APPENDIX A

WRITING THE VISION AND MAKING IT PLAIN ON CULTURAL BORDERS

I am indebted to Lovett Weems for many of these ideas of visioning from his book *Church Leadership,* including the quotation from Bishop Job (1993, p. 39).

WHAT IS A VISION?

- It is a dream.
- It is a picture of a preferred reality.
- "It is the gift of eyes of faith to see the invisible, to know the unknowable, to think the unthinkable, to experience the not yet. Vision allows us to see signs of the kingdom now in our midst." —Bishop Reuben P. Job
- It is the story or lens through which one sees reality.
- Vision is the imagination that gives inspiration and direction.

CHARACTERISTICS OF A VISION

1. A vision is related to mission, but different.

a. *Mission* is what we exist to do. For example, the mission of the church everywhere is to make disciples of all the nations. We could have the same generic mission statement for ten years.

b. *Vision* is what we see because we do what God is calling us to do in the immediate future—three to five years. It is by definition contemporary and specific. It is the preferred reality to which we are called. It focuses our energies and resources on those places where our giftedness and the world's needs converge.

2. A vision honors the past but focuses on the future, a preferred future.
3. A vision is both for others and for us. We and they can see outcomes, results, and contributions needed by all to have the vision come to fruit.
4. A vision is both realistic, rooted in the people who make up the organization and in the reality of the current situation, and lofty.
5. A vision takes the group to a new story.
6. A vision critiques the current picture and exposes the future picture to which we feel called.
7. A vision is a sign of hope.
8. A vision unites, energizes, focuses priorities, and serves as the ultimate standard. The vision is "the boss" of the church or system.
9. A vision raises sights and expectations; it invites and draws others in.
10. A vision opens the possibility of conflict with competing visions; it holds systems accountable and requires courage.

SOURCES FOR VISIONING

Identity: Who we have been historically, and who we are today.

Mission statement: States clearly and succinctly what we exist to do.

Values: How we do what we do; commitments, guidelines, boundaries within which we accomplish the mission.

Call: The reason we are here, our purpose, what God is calling us to do.

History: A history timeline points to important values, key events in the story; what are positive and negative implications for moving forward to the future?

Data from the internal environment: What do we need to know? How do we gather the information?

You will want information for the past five to ten years.
- Changes in church membership
- Changes in worship attendance
- Church school membership and attendance
- Budget growth or decline
- Membership demographics
- Sources of new members
- Participations in ministries

Data from the external environment: What do we need to know? How do we gather the information?

You will want information for the past five to ten years.
- Local population figures
- Racial, ethnic, and gender demographics
- School registration information
- Denominational and Judicatory membership an attendance
- Traffic pattern statistic
- Data from key community members and partners

Ministry by walking around: What do we see in our community? This helps us discern what God is calling us to.

Getting started: Exercises for small groups. (These can be used for the church board, the staff, or focus groups. This data I share as "the story we are beginning to tell." It becomes a text to exegete on the way to a vision and plan. This conversation works in a retreat format, or in a series of meetings.)

1. In five years, when we look around our church, we will see . . .
2. In your subgroups, listen to these texts and ask, "what does this say about God's vision for the church?" (These

are the texts that I use; you may use other texts that are key storylines for your congregation.)

Genesis 2:4–3:7	Isaiah 65:17-25
Amos 5:21-24	Exodus 3:1-14
Exodus 16:1-30	Matthew 28:16-20
Luke 1:26-38	

3. Which Bible story or image best speaks to the identity of our church (this is who we are)?
4. Imagine that the life of this church is an ongoing story. If you are writing *this* chapter in the story of this church, what is the title of it?
5. What is the title of the next chapter?
6. What are the key issues or plot points in the gap between this chapter and the next?
7. What will help write the next chapter and what will hinder it?
8. What is the story this community tells about us?
9. Finish this sentence: At our church, we say we want to _____, but I think we can do better at this.
10. If values are defined as the way we do what we do, make a list of the values you see lived out in this church and of how they are expressed in behaviors. In other words, by what norms do we live out our values?
11. If a vision is a picture of a preferred reality, what is your vision for this congregation? In other words, what is one thing God is calling us to, for such a time as this?
12. What do we need in order to do that, in terms of resources? Money? Staff? Volunteers? Space?
13. What will you do in order to make that happen?

CREATING THE CONTAINER FOR CHANGE

One of the key strategies that prepare people for change is to normalize that change is difficult and needs to be managed. Each year, I teach a course to leaders during Lent, so that we are having a common conversation and building a group story. My staff and consistory are mandated to come; team leaders, teachers, and those who want to be in leadership are strongly encouraged to come. We have had courses on Myers-Briggs Type and on emotional intelligence (what I know about myself and others); a course called *Race, Grace, and the Reign of God* (a conversation about race in the culture and racism in the church), a course called *Sex and the City* (a theological conversation about human sexuality), and a course on managing change.

Why People Resist Change

1. They feel out of control and powerless.
2. They wonder what it will mean for them.
3. People resist what they do not expect—tighten up when on the spot.
4. It disrupts routine; the known and certain are appealing (think Israel in the wilderness).
5. It makes people lose face, makes the past seem wrong.
6. It makes people feel uncertain about their competence.
7. There is a ripple effect on other people and efforts—it disrupts other things.
8. Things that are new are more work.
9. There is a chip on the shoulder from the past. People are mad at you for something else or at the organization or from some bad experience.
10. Sometimes the threat is real. Your great idea might hurt someone else. There are few totally positive ideas.

Adapted from Weems, 1993.

Ten Lessons to Be Learned about Change

1. Provide a clear picture of the change by sharing the vision.
2. Allow room for participation in the planning. Leave some choices.

3. Share information to the fullest extent possible, even if you do not have it all.
4. Divide change into small increments. Use pilot projects to test ideas.
5. Minimize surprises: communicate that change is coming.
6. Give people an opportunity to digest ideas.
7. Make people feel good about their competence. Praise sincerely and generously.
8. Reward the pioneer supporters—those out ahead of the curve.
9. Help people feel compensated for extra work, financially or with acknowledgments.
10. Try to redeem "losers" by letting them know early.

Adapted from Weems, 1993.

Nine Tips on Communicating the Vision to Deal with Change

1. Keep it simple.
2. Paint a verbal picture using metaphor, analogy, and example.
3. Use multiple forums—big and small meetings, memos and newsletters, bulletins and sermon series, formal and informal interaction.
4. Repeat the vision: ideas sink in only after they have been heard many times.
5. Lead by example: behavior from key people that is inconsistent with the vision overwhelms other communication.
6. Address and explain inconsistencies. Unaddressed inconsistencies undermine the credibility of all communication.
7. Listen and be listened to. Two-way communication is always more powerful than one-way communication.
8. Expect conflict. Conflict exists wherever there is more than one idea. It can be healthy. It must be addressed.

9. Create a container for conflict by being authentic, affirming the validity of feelings, allowing the group to hear all sides and decide together on the better idea.

Adapted from Weems, 1993.

Empowering People to Effect Change

1. Communicate a sensible vision to staff and congregation. A shared sense of purpose makes it easier to initiate actions to achieve that purpose.
2. Make structures and resources compatible with the vision. Unaligned structures and poorly aligned resources stop the flow of energy in the system.
3. Provide training for staff and leaders. Without the right skills and attitudes, people feel disempowered.
4. Align communication and staff to the vision. Poorly aligned communications and staff also stop the flow of energy in the system.
5. Confront staff and team leaders who undercut needed change.

Adapted from Kotter, 1996.

Building the Vision Team That Can Effect Change

Find the right people
  • With strong position power, broad expertise, and high credibility
  • With leadership and management, especially the former

Create trust
  • Through planned off-site events, play together!
  • With lots of talk and joint activities

Develop a common goal
  • Sensible to the head
  • Appealing to the heart

Then

- Treat everyone with respect
- Involve people
- Foster collaboration
- Strengthen others through sharing power
- Communicate!
- Be with people
- Recognize people
- Develop others
- Love the people

APPENDIX B

LEADERS ON THE BORDER: LIVING TEXTS PROTOCOL

Used with Clergy in the Study

The following may be useful in your context for assessing leaders.

Part I

Name
Date of birth
Where were you born?
Where did you grow up?
Birth order: _____ of _____siblings
What are/were your parents' names?
How old were they when you were born?
Occupations of parents
Describe your mother's parenting style in three words
Describe your father's parenting style in three words
Date you were ordained?
In which denomination?
You felt called to ministry when?
Denominational history
How long have you served this church?
Previous church leadership experience
Married or partnered? To whom? For how long?
Children? Ages?
Myers-Briggs Type

Part II

1. **Life chapters.** Think about your life as if it were a book. It is unfinished at this time but still contains interesting and well-defined chapters. Please divide your life into its major chapters and briefly describe each chapter. You may have as many or as few chapters as you like. Give each chapter a name, and describe what is in that chapter. Also, describe briefly the transition from one chapter to the next. Think of this as a general table of contents of the book.

2. **Ten key events or nuclear episodes.** We are going to move from the general to the specific now. I am going to ask you about ten key events in your life. By that I mean a specific happening, a critical incident, a significant episode in your past, set in a particular time and place. For example a conversation or a decision. I don't mean a whole summer vacation or a year in high school. Please describe the event and what this event says about who you are or were as a person.

- peak experience: the most wonderful moment in your life
- nadir experience: the worst moment in your life
- turning point: an episode wherein you underwent a significant change in your understanding of yourself—it doesn't matter if you knew it then; it is that you see it that way now
- earliest memory: one of the earliest memories you have that includes setting, scene, characters, feelings and thoughts—early is what is important here
- important childhood memory: any memory from your childhood, positive or negative, that stands out today
- important adolescent memory: same thing
- important adult memory: a stand-out memory from twenty-one on, again, same thing
- one other important memory: from long ago or recent past—again, positive or negative
- experiences relating to your race: one positive and one negative

• experiences relating to your gender: one positive and one negative

3. **Significant people.** (a) Your storied life is populated by a few significant people who have had a major impact on the narrative. Describe four of them; at least one should be someone to whom you are not related. Describe the kind of relationship you have or had with that person and the specific way he or she has had an impact on your story. (b) Tell me about your heroes or heroines.

4. **Future script.** Now let's talk about your future. Your story is not finished. I'd like you to describe your present dream, plan, or outline for the future story. We may think of the future story in terms of chapters also. Name the titles of the next chapters, and briefly describe them. How does your future story enable you (a) to be creative in the future and (b) to make a contribution to others?

5. **Stress and conflict.** Describe two areas in your life where there is significant stress, a major conflict, or a difficult problem or challenge that must be addressed. For each of the two, describe the nature of the stress, problem, or conflict in some detail, outlining the source of the concern, a brief history of its development and your plan, if you have one, for dealing with it in the future.

6. **Personal ideology, theology, and ethics.** Describe the way God relates to the world, in your view. Which images or stories about God most comfort you? Which images or stories about God most challenge you? Describe in a nutshell your core religious beliefs. In what ways are your beliefs different from those held by most people you know? How have your beliefs changed over time? Has there been any time of rapid change? How does what you believe affect how you live your life? Do you have a particular political orientation? What is the most important value in human living? What else do you want me to know about your most fundamental beliefs and values about God, life, and the world?

7. **Leader's interpretation.** Looking back over your entire life story as a book with chapters, episodes, and characters, you can discern a central theme, message, or idea that runs through the text. What is that major theme for your life? Please explain.

Part II Adapted, with permission, from Dan P. McAdams (1993).

APPENDIX C

LIVING TEXTS PROTOCOL: CONGREGATIONAL GROUPS

Please give short written answers to the following.

1. Why do you worship here at _____?
2. What is it that keeps you coming?
3. If you are writing a short identity statement about _____, what would it be?
4. What story do you imagine the community tells about your church?
5. What skills or capacities do congregants need when churches are multiracial and multicultural?
6. What skills or capacities do leaders need when churches are multiracial and multicultural?
7. What skills or capacities does your pastor have to lead this church?
8. What does your pastor do or say that teaches you about diversity?
9. How does your pastor handle boundaries? (truth telling? conflict? social justice?)
10. What is an example of a boundary (truth, conflict, social justice issue) _____has had to address?

STORYTELLING: CONVERSATION QUESTIONS: 60 MINUTES

1. If you had to tell one story that summarizes what your church is about, what is that story?
2. Tell a story of how the diversity at your church may have made you uncomfortable.
3. Tell a story about your pastor's leadership and why the story is important to this congregation.
4. How does your story connect to this congregation's story? Your pastor's story?
5. If you put your pastor's theology into one sentence, what would that be?
6. What holds this congregation together?
7. Is it more or less difficult to manage boundaries in this diverse community?

APPENDIX D

NEGOTIATING CULTURAL BOUND- ARIES CONVERSATION GROUP

While working on staff at the Alban Institute, I hosted a group of clergy and lay leaders in a conversation on negotiating cultural boundaries from April 2002 through May 2003. The group read articles and books and engaged in structured conversations about clergy leaders' work on the borders where diverse cultures intersect. These conversations supplemented my research, and helped me structure an Alban course entitled *Leading on the New Religious Frontier*. In addition to the capacities we described for leadership on the border, our other learnings are listed below.

LEARNINGS:

• Leaders on the border need allies in a support group; border leading can be lonely.
• Leaders on the border need to be willing to step over the edge.
• While pulling principles from our stories, we need to see that while our stories are different, some things carry over. If we can hone skills, we can get others to do so as well. Do we see ourselves as being self-revealing when we share border characteristics? Is there more than one way to be on the border?
• Language is important (for example, do we talk about the permanence of or pervasiveness of racism in America?).

- Post modernism means that various perspectives are valid. You can draw from many disciplines or sources and contribute to the discussion.
- We sometimes have to overcome internalized voices that whisper to us that we have nothing to contribute. People are listening in this context; how do I trust in other places that what I am saying is not being graded?
- Racism in America also makes whites question their voices.
- Even with difficulties trusting, the question is if not here, where? This is God's work; it is important.
- Border people need a binding vision. Passion allows you to do that work.
- It is sometimes a terrible liability being a white male with privilege.
- We need to consider the role of the faith community and the role of border people in eradicating racism.
- We need to consider the intersection of economics, race, and theology.

The Negotiating Cultural Boundaries Conversation Group
The Alban Institute
September 2002

APPENDIX E

THE PREACHER-LEADER-ARTIST

TRANSFORMING THE CHURCH THROUGH MULTIVOCAL STORYTELLING

1. There are many ways we can consider human development. One theory, or story, is that we are storied selves. Identity development is the process of finding one's own narrative voice amidst the speech of, and in dialogue with, others, as we interpret and make meaning of identity stories. We have complex, multiple identity-stories (for example, gender, sexual orientation, race, ethnicity, faith or religious traditions or belief systems). Therefore, we can think of identity as how these overlapping interweaving multitextured stories inform one another.

2. Call can be thought of as learning to discern and hear the voice that is the story that God is writing with us or has written for us. We can say that accepting our call means co-authoring that story with God and with our community. A call to ministry is a call to leadership.

3. Psychologist Howard Gardner says that leaders are those who tell compelling stories that effectively wrestle with the stories that already populate the minds of others. I agree and would add that the stories leaders tell are in part formed by their storied selves. So, the compelling stories preacher-leaders tell are affected by their identity-stories. As Fosters Brooks has said, preaching is truth through personality. I would say further that the vision the preacher-leaders bear is shaped by the vision they have of themselves, their

theology (their view of God acting in and for the world), and their hope in a picture of a preferred reality. For me that picture is best described as the reign of God.

4. To paraphrase L. Ron Hubbard, a society rises to the vision its artists articulate. Preaching articulates the vision of God's reign (the Word has made its dwelling place in the midst of us, even as the reign is about to be more fully manifest). Preacher-leaders are artists; every sermon is a work of art. Our work as homilists is to act as midwives to the birth of an idea rooted in the gospel.

5. Clergy and congregations are coauthoring a group identity, and a group call informed not only by the stories of leaders but also by members' stories and master stories (for example, the biblical narratives, binding narratives, like chosenness, vision, mission, and so on). The preacher-leader, then, is a *griot*—a storyteller or storyweaver who can exegete and make meaning of his or her own story, the congregation's emerging story, the stories of congregants and community members, and metanarratives. The preacher-leader-artist needs the capacity for multivocality—telling stories in multiple discourses, some of which are nonverbal.

6. Recall that one way to think about how we become a person is by introjecting the stories told to us and about us; in other words, we are storied selves. Identity development is the process of finding one's own narrative voice amidst the speech of and in dialogue with others. Thus, two goals of Christian education are (a) to offer the story of God's relationship to God's people as an identity story and (b) to facilitate the development of a theological voice in the self that can say, "this is how I make meaning of myself in relation to God, neighbor, and world." In other words, education is transformational as it answers the existential questions human beings address along the life cycle.

7. We have heard that one way to think of the learning process is as a five-point narrative journey from problem to an interlude for scanning to a moment of insight (ah ha!) to testing to a release of energy pent up around the problem or conflict (this is learning, and the Holy Spirit is the "teacher"). Thus, two objectives of Christian education are (a) to create a safe place, or container, in which the student can have an encounter with the Holy and (b) to leave enough space in the process for students to have an interlude of scanning in the process. In other words, delaying giving the answer allows students to build tension and yearn for the solution in such a way that learning is more profound.

8. We believe in the priesthood of all believers. The teacher-leader-artists help students discern their own calls to be the people of God more fully as they tell the compelling story of the gospel. They do this by being storytellers, or story-weavers, or storygleaners, or exegetes. Further, they are able to assist students in "finishing the story" for themselves and understanding its meaning (so what?) for self, congregation, community, and world.

9. Students bring their own unique stories to the encounter. They need to hear the gospel in the "language" that fits their experience. The arts allow for various discourses in which the good news can be shared. Painting, clay, and puppets speak to adults *and* children!

A NARRATIVE APPROACH TO PROBLEM SOLVING FOR LEADERS

A story has a beginning, a middle, and an end. Our stories are full of gaps that people must fill in order for the story to be performed. These gaps recruit the lived experience and the imagination of people. With every performance, people are reauthoring their lives. The evolution of lives is akin to the process of reauthoring, the process of people's entering into stories, taking them over, and making them their own. Thus, in two senses, the text analogy introduces us to an intertextual world. In the first sense, it proposes that people's lives are situated in texts within texts. In the second sense, every telling or retelling of a story, through its performance, is a new telling that encapsulates and expands upon the previous telling.

Adapted from White and Epston, 1990, p. 13.

Points to Consider

1. We are storied selves. Identity development is the process of finding one's own narrative voice amidst the speech of, and in dialogue with, others, as we interpret and make meaning of identity stories. We have complex, multiple identities (for example, gender, sexual orientation, race and ethnicity, religious traditions and belief systems and theo-ethics). Therefore, we can think of identity as how these overlapping interweaving multitextured stories inform one another.

2. Call or vocation can be thought of as hearing and discerning the story that God is writing with us or has written for us. Accepting our call means actively coauthoring that story with God and with our community. As Frederick Buechner says, call is "the place were your deep gladness and world's deep hunger meet."

3. Howard Gardner says that leaders are those who tell compelling stories that effectively wrestle with the stories that already populate the minds of others. I agree, and would add that the stories leaders tell are formed by their storied selves, and those stories help coauthor group identity or story. So, the vision/story leaders articulate is affected by their own vision/story (1995).

4. Congregations are coauthoring a community identity and story, a community sense of call, and community norms and

theo-ethics informed not only by the stories of leaders, but also by members' stories and master stories (for example, stories from culture, stories from history, biblical narratives). As Erik Erikson says, culture shapes the individual and the individual shapes culture.

SELECTED
BIBLIOGRAPHY

Primary Texts

Anzaldua, G. (1987). *Borderlands, la frontera.* San Francisco: Spinter/Aunt Lute.

Blount, B. and Tisdale, L. T. (Eds.) (2001). *Making room at the table: an invitation to multicultural worship.* Louisville: Westminster John Knox Press.

Clandinin, D. J., and F. M. Connelly (2000). *Narrative inquiry: Experience and story in qualitative research.* New York: John Wiley and Sons.

Davis, M., and D. Wallbridge (1981). *Boundary and space: An introduction to the work of D. W. Winnicott.* New York: Bruner/Mazel Publishers.

DeYoung, C. P. (1995). *Coming together: The Bible's message in an age of diversity.* Valley Forge, PA: Judson Press.

DeYoung, C. P., M. O. Emerson, G. Yancey, and K. C. Kim (2003). *United by faith: Multiracial congregations as a response to the racial divide.* New York: Oxford University Press.

DuBois, W. E. B. (1903). *The souls of black folk.* Chicago: A. C. McClurg.

Eakin, J. P. (1999). *How our lives become stories: Making selves.* Ithaca, NY: Cornell University Press.

Elizondo, V. (1983). *Galilean journey: The Mexican-American promise.* Maryknoll, NY: Orbis Books.

——— (2000). *The future is mestizo: Life where cultures meet.* Boulder: University of Colorado Press.

Ferdman, B. M. (2000). "Why am I who I am?" Constructing the cultural self in multicultural perspective. *Human Development,* Jan/Feb 2000.

Gardner, H. (1995). *Leading minds.* New York: Basic Books.

Gerkin, C. W. (1984). *The living human document: Re-visioning pastoral counseling in a hermeneutical mode.* Nashville: Abingdon Press.

Heifetz, R. A., (1994). *Leadership without easy answers.* Cambridge, MA: The Belnap Press of Harvard University.

Heifetz, R. A. and M. Linsky (2002). *Leadership on the line: Staying alive through the dangers of leading.* Boston: Harvard Business School Press.

Henderson, M. (1990). Speaking in tongues: Dialogics, dialectics, and the black woman writer's literary tradition. In H. Gates (Ed.), *Reading black, reading feminist* (pp. 116-142). New York: The Penguin Group.

Jones, J. (1991). The relational self: Contemporary psychoanalysis reconsiders religion. *Journal of the American Academy of Religion* 59: 119-135.

——— (1991). *Contemporary psychoanalysis and Religion: Transference and transcendence.* New Haven, CT: Yale University Press.

——— (1996). *Religion and psychology in transition: Psychoanalysis, feminism and theology.* New Haven, CT: Yale University Press.

Kotter, J. P. (1996). *Leading change.* Boston: Harvard Business School Press.

Levine, L. (1978). *Black culture and black consciousness: Afro-American thought from slavery to freedom.* London: Oxford Press.

Lewis, D. L. (1993). *W. E. B. DuBois: Biography of a race.* New York: Henry Holt and Company.

McAdams, D. P. (1993). *The stories we live by: Personal myths and the making of the self.* New York: The Guilford Press.

Schafer, R. (1992). *Retelling a life: Narration and dialogue in psychoanalysis.* New York: Basic Books.

Scharff, D. E. (1996). *Object relations theory and practice: An introduction.* Northvale, NJ: Jason Aronson, Inc.

Scharff, J. S. (1992). *Projective and introjective identification and the use of the therapist's self.* Northvale, NJ: Jason Aronson, Inc.

Smith, L. E. (1981). *Howard Thurman: The mystic as prophet.* Washington, DC: University Press of America.

Spence, D. P. (1982). *Narrative truth and historical truth: Meaning and interpretation in psychoanalysis.* New York: W.W. Norton & Company.

Tatum, B. D. (1997). *"Why are all the black kids sitting together in the cafeteria?" And other conversations about race.* New York: Basic Books.

Thandeka (2000). *Learning to be white: Money, race, and God in America.* New York: Continuum.

Thurman, H. (1954). *The creative encounter: An interpretation of religion and the social witness.* Richmond, IN: Friends United Press.

———— (1965). *The luminous darkness: A personal interpretation of the anatomy of segregation and the ground of hope.* New York: Harper & Row.

———— (1971). *The search for common ground: An inquiry into the basis of man's experience of community.* New York: Harper & Row.

———— (1979). *With head and heart: The autobiography of Howard Thurman.* New York: Harcourt Brace Jovanovich.

Ulanov, A. B. (2001). *Finding space: Winnicott, God, and psychic reality.* Louisville: Westminster John Knox Press.

White, M., and D. Eptson (1990). *Narrative means to therapeutic ends.* New York: W.W. Norton & Company.

Winnicott, D. W. (1965). *The maturational processes and the facilitating environment: Studies in the theory of emotional development.* Madison, CT: International Universities Press.

———— (1971). *Playing and reality.* London: Routledge.

———— (1986). *Home is where we start from: Essays by a psychoanalyst.* New York: W.W. Norton & Company.

———— (1989). *Psychoanalytic explorations.* Cambridge, MA: Harvard University Press.

Secondary Texts

Angrosino, M. V. (2001). *Talking about cultural diversity in your church: Gifts and challenges.* Walnut Creek, CA: Rowman and Littlefield Publishers.

Appiah, K. A. (1994). Identity, authenticity, survival: Multicultural societies and social reproduction. In C. Taylor (Ed.), *Multiculturalism.* Princeton, NJ: Princeton University Press.

———— (1998). The limits of pluralism. In A. M. Melzer, J. Weinberger, and M. R. Zinman (Eds.), *Multiculturalism and American democracy.* Lawrence: University of Kansas Press.

———— (1999). Race, culture and identity: Misunderstood connections. In K. A. Appiah and A. Gutmann (Eds.), *Color conscious: The political morality of race.* Chicago: University of Chicago Press.

Barndt, J. (1991). *Dismantling racism: The continuing challenge to white America.* Minneapolis: Augsburg.

Brown, L. S. (1995). Anti-racism as an ethical norm in feminist therapy practice. In J. Adleman and G. Enguidanos (Eds.), *Racism in the lives of women: Testimony, theory and guides to antiracist practice* (pp. 137-148). New York: The Haworth Press.

Butler, L. H. (1994). *African American identity formation: An Eriksonian approach.* Unpublished doctoral dissertation, Drew University, Madison, NJ.

Cannon, K. G. (1988). *Black womanist ethics.* Atlanta: Scholars Press.

Capps, D. (1998). *Living stories: Pastoral counseling in congregational context.* Minneapolis: Fortress Press.

Carter, R. T. (1995). *The influence of race and racial identity in psychotherapy: Toward a racially inclusive model.* New York: John Wiley and Sons.

Chaves, M. (1999). *How do we worship?* Bethesda, MD: The Alban Institute.

Chodorow, N. (1989). *Feminism and psychoanalytic theory.* New Haven, CT: Yale University Press.

Christian, B. (1985). *Black feminist criticism.* New York: Pergamon Press.

Collins, P. H. (1998). *Fighting words: Black women and the search for justice.* Minneapolis: University of Minnesota Press.

Comas-Diaz, L., and B. Greene (Eds.) (1994). *Women of color: Integrating ethnic and gender identities in psychotherapy.* New York: Guilford Press.

Cross, W. E., Jr. (1995). In search of blackness and afrocentricity: The psychology of black identity change. In H. W. Harris, E. C. Blue and E. E. H. Griffith (Eds.), *Racial and ethnic identity: Psychological development and creative expression* (pp. 53-72). New York: Routledge.

Diamond, M. A., and G. B. Adams (1999). The psychodynamics of ethical behavior in organizations. *The American Behavioral Scientist,* 245-261.

Early, G. (Ed.) (1993). *Lure and loathing: Essays on race, identity, and the ambivalence of assimilation.* New York: Allen Lane.

Eck, D. L. (2001). *A new religious America: How a Christian country has become the world's most religiously diverse nation.* San Francisco: Harper Collins.

Emerson, M.O., and C. Smith (2000). *Divided by faith: Evangelical religion and the problem of race in America.* New York: Oxford University Press.

Erikson, E. H. (1950). *Childhood and society.* New York: W.W. Norton & Company.

———— (1968). *Identity, youth and crisis.* New York: W.W. Norton & Company.

Fanon, F. (1967). *Black skin, white masks.* New York: Grove Press.

Felder, C. H. (1989). *Troubling biblical waters: Race, class and family.* Maryknoll, NY: Orbis Books.

———— (1993). Recovering multicuturalism in scripture. In C. H. Felder (Ed.), *The original African heritage study Bible.* Nashville: The James C. Winston Publishing Company.

Ferdman, B. M. (2000). Constructing the cultural self in multicultural perspective. *Human Development,* Jan/Feb 2000, 19-23.

Fluker, W. E. (1989). *They looked for a city: A comparative analysis of the ideal of community in the thought of Howard Thurman and Martin Luther King, Jr.* Lanham, MD: University Press of America.

Fong, B. W. (1996). *Racial equality in the church: a critique of the homogenous unit principle in light of a practical theology perspective.* Lanham, MD: University Press of America, Inc.

Foster, C. (1997). *Embracing diversity: Leadership in multicultural congregations.* Bethesda, MD: The Alban Institute.

Foster, C., and T. Brelsford (1996). *We are the church together: Cultural diversity in congregational life.* Valley Forge, PA: Trinity Press International.

Frable, D. E. S. (1997). Gender, racial, ethnic, sexual and class identities. *Annual Review of Psychology,* Palo Alto.

Gates, H. L., Jr. (1992). *Loose canons: Notes on cultural wars.* New York: Oxford University Press.

———— (1998). *The signifying monkey: Theory of African-American literary criticism.* New York: Oxford Press.

Gilligan, C. (1982). *In a different voice.* Cambridge, MA: Harvard University Press.

González, J. L. (1992). *Out of every tribe and nation: Christian theology at the ethnic roundtable.* Nashville: Abingdon Press.

Greene, B. (1994). Diversity and difference: Race and feminist psychotherapy. In M. P. Merkin (Ed.), *Women in context: Toward a feminist reconstruction of psychotherapy.* New York: The Guilford Press.

Helms, J. E. (Ed.) (1990). *Black and white racial identity: Theory, research, and practice.* Westport, CT: Greenwood Press.

hooks, b. (1990). *Yearnings: Race, gender, and cultural politics.* Boston: South End Press.

———— (1992). *Black looks: Race and representation.* Boston: South End Press.

Howard, G. S. (1991). Culture tales: A narrative approach to thinking, cross-cultural psychology and psychotherapy. *American Psychologist, 46*(3), 187-197.

Ikenye, N. J. B. (2001). The development of a bicultural personality for Christian ministries. *Anglican Theological Review, Fall, 2001,* 793-820.

Isasi-Diaz, A. M. (1990). The Bible and mujerista theology. In S. B. Thistlewaite and M. P. Engel (Eds.), *Lift every voice: Constructing Christian theologies from the underside.* San Francisco: Harper Collins.

Jacobs, J. L., and D. Capps (1997). *Religion, society and psychoanalysis: Readings in psychoanalytic theory.* Oxford: Westview Press.

Jimoh, A. Y. (1998). Double consciousness, modernism, and womanist themes in Gwendolyn Brooks's "The Anniad." *Melus* 167-186.

Knight, M. G. (2000). Ethics in qualitative research: Multicultural feminist activist research. *Theory Into Practice.*

Kohut, H. (1971). *The analysis of the self: A systematic approach to the psychoanalytic treatment of narcissistic personality disorders.* Madison, WI: International Universities Press, Inc.

———— (1977). *The restoration of the self.* Madison, WI: International Universities Press, Inc.

Krebs, N. B. (2002). *Edge Walkers: Defusing culture on the new global frontier.* Far Hills, NJ: New Horizon Press.

Kujawa-Holbrook, S. (2002). *A house of prayer for all peoples: Congregations building multiracial community.* Bethesda, MD: The Alban Institute.

Kvale, S. (1999). The psychoanalytic interview as qualitative research. *Qualitative Inquiry,* March.

Lacan, J. (1977). *Écrits: A selection.* New York: W.W. Norton & Company.

Law, E. H. F. (1993). *The wolf shall dwell with the lamb: spirituality for leadership in a multicultural community.* St. Louis: Chalice Press.

———— (1996). *The bush was blazing but not consumed.* St. Louis, MO: Chalice Press.

Lorde, A. (1984). *Sister outsider: Essays and speeches by Audre Lorde.* Freedom, CA: The Crossing Press.

McDargh, J. (1983). *Psychoanalytic object relations theory and the study of religion.* Lanham, MD: University Press of America.

Meissner, W. W. (1984). *Psychoanalysis and religious experience.* New Haven: Yale University Press.

Mitchell, S., and M. Black (Eds.) (1995). *Freud and beyond: A history of modern psychoanalytic thought.* New York: Basic Books.

Ogden, T. (1997). *Reverie and interpretation: Sensing something human.* Northvale, NJ: Jason Aronson.

O'Hanrahan, B. (2001). *The effect of leader statements on patterns of group development in small study groups of a Tavistock group relations conference.* Temple University, unpublished dissertation.

Okholm, D. L. (Ed.) (1997). *The gospel in black and white: Theological resources for racial reconciliation.* Downers Grove, IL: InterVarsity Press.

Peart, N. A. (2000). *Separate no more: Understanding and developing racial reconciliation in your church.* Grand Rapids, MI: Baker Books.

Perry, P. (2001). White means never having to say you're ethnic. *Journal of Contemporary Ethnography,* Feb 2001, 59-61.

Rappaport, J. (2000). Community narratives: Tales of terror and joy. *American Journal of Community Psychology.* February.

Rizzuto, A. (1979). *The birth of the living God: A psychoanalytic study.* Chicago: University of Chicago Press.

Shorter-Gooden, K. (2002). Qualitative methods: An essential tool for multicultural psychology. In E. Savis-Russell (Ed.), *The California school of professional psychology handbook of multicultural education, research, intervention and training* (pp. 123-138). San Francisco: Jossey-Bass.

Skura, M. (1981). *The literary use of the psychoanalytic process.* New Haven: Yale University Press.

Sue, D. W., and D. Sue (1999). *Counseling the culturally different: Theory and practice.* New York: John Wiley and Sons.

Sugirtharajah, R. S. (1991). *Voices from the margin: Interpreting the Bible in the third world.* Maryknoll, NY: Orbis Books.

Suzuki, L. A., M. Prendes-Lintel, L. Wertlieb, and A. Stallings (1999). Exploring multicultural issues using qualitative methods. In *Using Qualitative Methods in Psychology.* Thousand Oaks, CA: Sage Publications.

SELECTED BIBLIOGRAPHY

Tatum, B. D. (1999). Which way do we go? Leading for diversity in the new frontier. *The Journal of Negro Education,* Fall, 550-554.

Tugendhat, E. (1993). The role of identity in the constitution of morality. In G. Noam and T. Wren (Eds.), *The moral self* (pp. 3-15). Cambridge, MA: The MIT Press, 1993, pp. 3-15.

Unander, D. (2000). *Shattering the myth of race: Genetic realities and biblical truths.* Valley Forge, PA: Judson Press.

Weems, L. (1993). *Church leadership: Vision, team, culture and integrity.* Nashville: Abingdon Press.

Welsing, F. C. (1991). *The Isis papers: The keys to the colors.* Chicago: Third World Press.

West, T. (1999). *Wounds of the spirit: Black women, violence, and resistance ethics.* New York: New York University Press.

NOTES

1. Stories and Living Texts

1. Howard Gardner, author of *Leading Minds* (1995), argues that leaders tell compelling stories that wrestle with the story already in the minds of followers.
2. Inspired by my colleague Brian Blount, who speaks about how the reign of God breaks in through Jesus' preaching, teaching, and healing ministry (see *Go Preach!*), I think of the preaching and teaching ministries of church leaders as effectively rehearsing the Reign of God and creating a pocket of promise in which the not-yet is realized now.
3. Howard Gardner, David Shafer, and Donald Scharff help me to understand stories this way.
4. Donald Winnicott and other object relations theorists talk about development in terms of the environment in which a person develops. Ronald Heifetz uses the same term for that, the container, to describe the environments that leaders create in order to facilitate change.
5. Race and ethnicity, gender, and class are three complicated identity components that significantly affect the quality of life experienced in American culture. They are *storied* or given meaning by the culture. Black feminist and womanist scholars across disciplines (West, 1999; Collins, 1990; Greene, 1992; Pinderhughes, 1989; Townes, 1993; hooks, 1989, 1992; Lorde, 1984) inform my analysis. I am using the terms *racial* and *ethnic* to describe what most Americans would call *race*. There is only one race, the human race, but the physical characteristics of the differences in ethnicities get racialized and colorized in America.
6. Elizondo and others suggest that Jesus' racial/ethnic identity was *Mestizo* or mixed as well. See Cain H. Felder (1989, 1991, 1992); Curtiss DeYoung (1995); Kelly Brown Douglass (1994); R. S. Sugirtharajah (1993). For me, the multicultural and multiracial identity of the historic Jesus is a liberating fact, just as important as his poor, humble beginnings. God used an

unlikely agent to work God's wonders in the world; it is a strategy that God has used repeatedly.

7. For an excellent exegesis of Jesus as a border crosser in the Temple of Jerusalem, see Brian Blount's essay "The Apocalypse of Worship: A House of Prayer for ALL the Nations" (2001). In B. Blount and N. Tubbs Tisdale (Eds.), *Making Room at the Table: An Invitation to Multicultural Worship* (pp. 16-29). Louisville: Westminster John Knox Press.

8. From an object relations perspective, the pre-oedipal relationships between the developing self and the objects with whom it relates are the beginning of personality development. Whereas some object relations theorists focus on introjective and projective dynamics between the infant and the caregiver (Fairbairn, 1952; Klein, 1975; Bion, 1962), Winnicott focuses more on the environment the caregiver creates.

9. In Gloria Anzaldua's discussion of the new mestiza in *Borderlands/La Frontera: The New Mestiza*, her sense of being a *border person* includes "straddling" not only the Texas/Mexican border, but also other psychological, sexual, and spiritual borderlands that are present "whenever two or more cultures edge each other" (Anzaldua, 1987, p. iii).

2. Storying an Ethic of Truth Telling and Social Justice

1. Donald Winnicott and other object relations theorists talk about development in terms of the environment in which a person develops. Ronald Heifetz uses the same term for that, the container, to describe the environments that leaders create in order to facilitate change.

2. For an excellent comparison of object relations theories, see David E. Scharff, *Object Relations Theory and Practice: An Introduction* (Northvale: Jason Aronson, Inc., 1996). For a comprehensive treatment of the development of the theories, see J. R. Greenburg and S. A. Mitchell, *Object Relations in Psychoanalytic Theory* (Cambridge, MA: Harvard University Press, 1983).

3. Winnicott credits Jacques Lacan with the idea of the mirror stage. In a lecture delivered in 1949 to the sixteenth international congress of psychoanalysis, in Zurich, Lacan stated that identification is "the transformation that takes place in the subject when

he assumes an image" (*Ecrits: A Selection,* 1977, W.W. Norton, p. 2).

4. Winnicott calls that compliance a false self. There are various levels of false self in his theory, from relatively healthy to pathological. It is difficult to not communicate a sense of inauthenticity while using the term false. For our purposes, I will use other-conscious to describe the relative adaptation that happens when a developing self learns early to be overconcerned about the gaze of the other.

5. For Winnicott's discussion on degrees of false self, see "Ego Distortion in Terms of True and False Self" (1960) in *The Maturational Processes and the Facilitating Environment: Studies in the Theory of Emotional Development* (International Universities Press, 1965, pp. 149-152).

6. I am imagining how I might theorize about both extreme compliance (what some would pejoratively call being a "Tom" or an "oreo," or extremely racist, sexist, heterosexist behavior as protecting the true self. For example, is it logical that a false self would hate another human being to protect the true self from vulnerability, exposure, or the need to let go of power? Along the continuum would be various levels of compliance, with various levels of true and false self-development.

7. Elizondo says that Jesus was rumored to be the "child of a Jewish girl and a Roman father ... he appeared to be a half-breed" (Elizondo, 2000, p. 79). See also Cain Hope Felder.

8. I am referring here to Mae Henderson's trope for multivocality—glossalia and heteroglossia—in her essay "Speaking in Tongues" (1990). Dr. Henderson's analysis will be used as a lens through which to exegete leaders' and congregational stories in chapter 4.

9. Randolph shared stories about his younger brother who is also an Episcopal priest.

3. *Storying an Ethic of Conflict and Border Crossing: Learning from Leaders*

1. An octoroon was someone with 1/8 of his or her lineage traced to people from the African diaspora.

2. As James Jones notes, "The child's experience with transitional objects is neither objective or subjective. Instead transitional

experience can be called interactional, for it begins to form in the interactional space between the mother and the infant. Good enough care-taking provides the infant with enough trust in life's dependability that development is not thwarted and the infant can venture beyond the perimeter of his or her private world" (Jones, 1996, p. 133).

3. As Ann Ulanov helpfully offers, "The space of playing offers us rest from the daunting ego-task of trying to keep together outward reality and inward wishes and hopes. In the spaces in between, we take time-off; we meander happily" (A. Ulanov, *Finding Space: Winnicott, God and Psychic Reality*, 2001, p. 15).

4. See Jones, 1991; McDargh, 1983; Rizzuto, 1981; Ulanov, 2001.

5. For an excellent discussion of transformation from a narrative perspective, see James Loder's (1982) *The Transforming Moment: Understanding Convictional Experiences* (New York: Helmers and Howard).

6. This is what Heinz Kohut (1971, 1977) refers to as empathy.

7. It is Melanie Klein who emphasizes splitting of objects between good and bad. See (1986) "A Study of Envy and Gratitude," from *The Selected Melanie Klein*, (Ed.) J. Mitchell (London: Hogarth Press; New York: The Free Press, Macmillan), pp. 211-29.

4. Stories on the Border: Told in Multiple Voices

1. Black women are not alone in the ability/necessity to speak in a multiplicity of discourses. In her seminal text, *Borderlands/La Frontera: The New Mestiza*, Chicana feminist Gloria Anzaldua switches in language "codes" from English to Castilian Spanish to "Tex-Mex" to Nahuatl to a mixture of all of these in what she calls the "language of the Borderlands" (1987). By asserting a *mestiza*, or mixed consciousness, she seeks to break down dualistic hegemonic paradigms. In other words, she advocates for "both/and ... but" consciousness in order to break through the binary, either/or thinking that puts human beings in oppressive boxes.

2. See the model of multicultural and multiracial congregational development in appendix E.

3. Henderson refers to plural identity as "subjective plurality that finally allows [black women writers] to become an expressive

site for a dialectics/dialogics of identity and difference" (Henderson, 1995, p. 137).

4. This data was gathered in congregational interviews. See appendix C.

5. White and Epston (1990) use *"to story"* as a verb.

6. Writing about black preaching, Lawrence Levine says that preachers are *boundary extenders*; they create "a new world by transcending the narrow confines of the one in which they were forced to live. They extended the boundaries backward until it fused with the world of the Old Testament, and upward until it became one with the world beyond" (Levine, 1978).

5. Enacting the Pentecost Paradigm

1. All leaders who accept the moral challenge to add greater cultural diversity to their workforces must engage in what James McGregor Burns calls transformational leadership, which elevates followers to a higher moral level. See "The Structure of Moral Leadership" in Burns, *Leadership,* chapter 2 (1978).

2. This is in contrast to technical leadership challenges, which require authorities to apply current know-how to solve problems such as which copier to purchase. Based on Heifetz's definition, the leaders in our study are attempting to do adaptive work in their local church and in society.

3. Heifetz acknowledges that he borrows the term *holding environment* from psychoanalytic understandings of the parent's relationship to the child and the therapist's relationship to the client (1994, p. 104). For Heifetz, "a holding environment consists of any relationship in which one party has the power to hold the attention of another party and facilitate adaptive work" (pp. 104-5). A holding environment "contains and regulates stresses that work generates" (p. 105). Trust is a critical component of holding. See Winnicott's concept of "belief in" and Erik Erikson's trust versus mistrust. Rituals, like the Eucharist or baptism, and liturgy and prayer are all holding environments in which the work of transforming the world to what it can be may take place. These containers help individuals negotiate internal conflict and intra-personal conflict, as they learn to deal with change.

4. The Spiral of Deepening Relationships is contrasted with continuums in multiracial/multicultural congregational development (Peart, 2000; Crossroads Ministries). Deepening relationships move congregations from superficial coexistence to real, authentic community. Whereas the predominant direction of the spiral is down and deep, stories overlap and weave in such ways that places on the spiral might be revisited.

CPSIA information can be obtained at www.ICGtesting.com
Printed in the USA
BVOW06s2255210916

462868BV00004B/5/P